BRITISH AND AMERICAN WOMEN AT WORK

Do Equal Opportunities Policies Matter?

Shirley Dex
and
Lois B. Shaw

MACMILLAN

First published 1986

Published by
THE MACMILLAN PRESS LTD
Houndmills, Basingstoke, Hampshire RG21 2XS
and London
Companies and representatives
throughout the world

Printed in Hong Kong

British Library Cataloguing in Publication Data
Dex, Shirley
British and American Women at Work: do equal opportunities policies matter?
1. Women—Employment   2. Sex discrimination in employment
I. Title   II. Shaw, Lois Banfill
331.4'133   HD6060
ISBN 0-333-40219-7 (hardcover)
ISBN 0-333-40220-0 (paperback)

Contents

Tables and Figures

TABLES

FIGURES

Acknowledgements

The Equal Opportunities Commission in Britain funded the research contained in this volume. We particularly wish to thank Ed Puttick and other staff at the EOC for their help and encouragement in carrying out this project. The views expressed in this book are those of the authors and not necessarily those of the Equal Opportunities Commission.

We thank Mary Gagen and Pan-Long Tsai for their assistance in the analysis of the NLS data; Jean Martin, Peter Elias and Brian Main who provided help with the WES analysis; Kim Pickerill who produced the typescript; Heather Joshi who made useful comments and corrected several errors.

SHIRLEY DEX
LOIS B. SHAW

Abbreviations and Terms Used

ABBREVIATIONS

AFDC	Aid to Families with Dependent Children (USA)
EEO	Equal Employment Opportunities (USA)
EEOC	Equal Employment Opportunities Commission (USA)
EOC	Equal Opportunities Commission (GB)
FCC	Federal Contract Compliance (USA)
NLS	National Longitudinal Surveys of Labor Market Experience (USA)
NUT	National Union of Teachers (GB)
OFCC	Office of Federal Contract Compliance (USA)
OLS	Ordinary least squares
OPCS	Office of Population Censuses and Surveys (UK)
WES	Women and Employment Survey (GB)

TERMS

American	refers to the United States of America
Britain	refers to Great Britain
Working, not working	refers to paid employment or the lack of paid employment. This usage is to be consistent with other analyses of our data.

1 Introduction

Since the introduction of equal opportunities policies in Britain and in the USA researchers have tried to assess their impact both on women and, in the USA, on minority groups. Research has tended to focus on assessing the impact of the legislation on women's earnings within that country by making before and after comparisons and controlling for other changes which might have been taking place concurrently. Since much of the legislation focuses on equal pay and earnings this is not surprising. This type of research has produced equivocal results in Britain and the USA. Some results suggest that the legislation has improved women's earnings, others that it has had little effect. The Equal Opportunities Commission in Britain provided us with funding to explore a different approach to this issue.

We have set out to offer an alternative approach to this question of how successful equal opportunities policies are for women. The approach is essentially one of comparison between British and American women. Whilst there are similarities in the equal opportunities legislation of Britain and the USA there are also differences which means that comparative work provides the opportunity to explore the impact of the differences. Adopting a comparative approach means that the focus can be broadened to include an examination of all the policies which have a bearing on women's employment; policies on taxation, child-care provisions and maternity leave thus become part of our concern. In addition we intend to focus not on earnings but on women's occupational status. It is well established that much of women's inferior position in the labour market is a result of their segregated occupational status rather than being paid less than men for doing the same jobs. It seems entirely appropriate therefore that a test of the effects of equal opportunities policies should be made using women's occupational status; in any case women's occupations in large part determine their earnings. Such an approach also involves us in assessing the extent to which any structural differences in our two economies have an impact on women's opportunities.

1

Cross-cultural comparative work is rare. Research has often been constrained by the lack of suitable data. The availability of data on women's employment which permitted direct comparisons provided a rare opportunity to pursue this question. More often, comparisons are restricted to using published statistics from each country which are based often on different definitions (Meehan, 1985). The success of this test of equal opportunities policies also relies upon the availability of information on women's working experiences over time – longitudinal or work-history data. Such data became available in Britain only recently in 1980 with the collection by the Department of Employment and Office of Population Censuses and Surveys of the Women and Employment Survey (WES). The USA has had large-scale longitudinal data on women's working experiences since 1967–8 with the initiation of the National Longitudinal Surveys of Labor Market Experience (NLS). It has been possible to make some direct comparisons between British and American women over the period 1967 to 1980 using these two sources. We have focused our attention on women's experiences over the period of family formation to examine the effects of childbirth and child-rearing on women's labour-market experiences. Since this period is traditionally one in which women are thought to lose ground in terms of their employment prospects it is interesting to see what impact equal opportunities policies have at this phase of women's experiences. The information contained in these two surveys allows us to compare the time spent out of work over childbirth, the patterns of employment over family formation, occupational and industrial changes at this time, child-care provisions and other aspects of women's work histories. These comparisons will be set against the background of the differences in legislation and policy provisions pertaining to women's employment in Britain and the USA, and against the structural differences in the two economies. We conclude that equal opportunities policies have had an impact on women's employment prospects, but policies on child-care provision have probably had a bigger impact, and the differing structures of employment opportunities for women in the two countries have also had a role to play.

In the rest of this chapter we describe the relevant legislation and policies which have a bearing on women's employment in Britain and the USA. We also review the research testing the effects of legislation on earnings in the two countries. Some of the details about the data sources for our comparisons are also provided. The technical aspects of the comparison are provided in Appendix A.

EQUAL OPPORTUNITIES LEGISLATION

Both Britain and the USA have legislation against sex discrimination in employment although the enforcement of the law differs in the two countries as does the extent to which equal opportunities are promoted. In Britain, the Equal Pay Act was passed in 1970 to come into effect in 1975. The Act was designed to prevent inequalities in the terms and conditions of employment between men and women. It does not ensure equality of opportunity in access to jobs, however. The Equal Pay Act stipulated that men and women are to be paid the same amount if they are employed in the same or broadly similar work. This left considerable room for debate over what counted as 'broadly similar'. Since 1 January 1984 the law has clarified the grounds upon which individuals can claim equal pay for work of equal value (EOC, 1984). The Sex Discrimination Act was passed in Britain in 1975 and it prohibits discrimination in respect of hiring, opportunities for promotion, transfer and training, and dismissal procedures on grounds of gender or marriage. The Act protects married persons of either sex, single women and single men separately, and precludes both direct and indirect discrimination. Indirect discrimination is said to occur mainly where a requirement or condition is equally applicable to men and women, but is such that the proportion of women who are able to comply with the requirement is considerably smaller than the proportion of men who can comply. The Act applies equally for men and women and therefore makes reverse discrimination in favour of women generally unlawful, except in the area of women's training facilities. Under both these provisions the individual can take a case against his or her employer and the burden of proof is on the complainant to show that discrimination has taken place. An Equal Opportunities Commission was set up alongside the legislation to improve and monitor the relative position of women.

In the USA an Equal Pay Act was passed in 1963 which prohibited sex discrimination in salaries when men and women are employed in the same jobs or in jobs which are substantially (not identically) equal in skill, effort, responsibility and working conditions. Other legislation outlawing sex discrimination was part of the 1964 Civil Rights Act (Title VII) and is therefore of longer standing than the equivalent British legislation. Title VII was a far-ranging and comprehensive federal law prohibiting discrimination in all aspects of employment such as hiring, firing, compensation, terms, conditions, privileges of employment, training, retraining and apprenticeship. An Equal Employment Opportunity Commission was set up in the late 1960s to enforce the 1964 Act. Enforcement of Title VII is a function of the Equal Employment Opportunity Commission (EEOC). The EEOC investigates charges of unlawful employment practices, and if it determines that there is reasonable cause to believe that discrimination has occurred, the EEOC attempts to resolve the problem through conciliation. If conciliation fails, either the employee or the EEOC may bring a suit against the employer. Class action suits may be brought and these obviously have wider-ranging implications. Therefore, under legislation in the USA, the individual often has the backing of a government agency in pursuing a claim. Well-publicised settlements involving thousands of employees, such as the American Telephone and Telegraph case (see Wallace, 1976) have undoubtedly caused many large companies to revise their employment practices. Class action suits are also thought to have been particularly effective.

The Act was amended in 1972 and subsequently by a series of Titles which have extended its range and coverage, outlawing discrimination in employment-related areas – for example, maternity leave. The net effect of these amendments, as most commentators seem to agree, is that equal opportunities legislation is more extensive in the USA. Cases of discrimination have been more aggressively pursued through the courts in the USA than in Britain. The legislation in the USA involved a clause for outlawing indirect discrimination which influenced the British legislation. The most notable difference between British and US legislation is that, unlike Britain, the USA has introduced affirmative action provisions in the Executive Orders 11246 (1965) and 11375 (1967) administered by the OFCC (Office of Federal Contract Compliance). These provisions require certain firms to set goals and timetables for increasing the employment of all minority workers, including women, in the various levels of the organisation. Firms who have or want federal contracts are obliged to adopt these practices.

The combination of affirmative action and the greater frequency of sex discrimination cases make the USA a more aggressive pursuer of equal opportunities for women than Britain. This is the climate in the context of which our comparisons are set and it is important to remember that the USA also has approximately a ten-year start over Britain with respect to this legislation. Meehan (1985) has provided a useful comparison of the political processes by which this legislation came to be passed in Britain and the USA. For the period covered by our surveys, the American legislation is likely to have had a significant impact on the American women in the sample. The effect on the British women is likely to be much less since the legislation was enacted in the middle of this period. We will review the studies which have attempted to quantify the effects of these policies on women's earnings later in this chapter.

MATERNITY BENEFITS

Britain has a national scheme for providing women with paid time off work for childbirth which was introduced as part of the Employment Protection Act of 1975. This Act gave women the right to reinstatement, maternity pay and protection from unfair dismissal. The provisions concerning the right to reinstatement were modified by the Employment Act of 1980. The maternity-leave legislation sets out the statutory minimum provisions but individual employers can agree with their employees to provide better schemes and in fact some private maternity-leave schemes were in operation prior to this legislation. To be eligible for maternity leave under the statutory provisions, a woman must fulfil a number of conditions; if she works 16 hours or more per week she must have been with the same employer for at least 104 weeks before the beginning of the eleventh week before confinement; if she works between 8 and 16 hours per week, to be eligible she must have worked with the same employer for five years or more. Very small employers are exempt from the scheme. A woman must notify her employer of her intention to return and she is then eligible to have eleven antenatal weeks off work before the childbirth and twenty-nine post-natal weeks off work. She will receive six weeks pay at 90 per cent of normal earnings. In their comparison of maternity benefits throughout Europe Davidson and Cooper (1983) suggest that Britain has lower pay and stricter conditions for eligibility than other European countries. The date at which statutory provisions were introduced in Britain means that many of the women in our sample, especially the older women, would have been unable to benefit from the scheme.

The United States is notable for being the only major industrialised country in the world without a national insurance plan covering medical expenses for childbirth and it is one of the few industrialised countries that does not provide any statutory cash benefits to women over childbirth to compensate them for lost earnings. It is not uncommon for private employers in the USA to have maternity benefit schemes, however. In fact the NLS is a major source of information on the extent of such schemes since no employer surveys are available. Also, after the 1964 Civil Rights Act, three States voluntarily passed legislation requiring employers to pay disability benefits to women for maternity leave. Since the late 1960s, the EEOC in the USA began to agitate for better provisions by arguing that maternity provisions should be treated in the same way as other physical disability benefits. Some progress was made with individual companies, but a series of US Supreme Court decisions on pregnancy disability undermined this position, as reported in Adams and Winston (1980, pp. 34–5). A bill introduced in 1978 finally outlawed a list of discriminatory practices with the effect of entitling pregnant employees to the same benefits enjoyed by other disabled employees with the exception of medical coverage and sick leave for abortion. However, the bill fell far short of creating a nationally-sponsored maternity leave scheme. This recent scheme was too late to affect the women in our sample, to any great extent, up to their 1980 interview. In 1978 about 20 per cent of employed women in the NLS young women's sample reported that their employers provide paid maternity leave; another 25 per cent said that unpaid leave was available.

Neither Britain nor the USA have many paternity leave provisions. A recent study in Britain by Bell *et al.* (1983) illustrates that paternity leave does exist in Britain although it is far from being widespread.

CHILD CARE

The provision for child care is on a very *ad hoc* basis in both Britain and the USA. There are no uniform government-sponsored schemes of child care in either country. A wide variety of types of provision exist in the two countries but in total they are not sufficient to provide care for the children of all families with working mothers, even if there were no other prohibitive circumstances. There is more information available on child care in the USA than there is in Britain but the need for better information has been noted in both countries (Bone, 1977; Browne, 1984). Fortunately, our two surveys asked comparable questions on the types of child care which women used and they are thus a major source of information on the subject. The results reported in Chapter 2 show that there is considerable varia-

tion between Britain and the USA, with paid care outside the home
being more commonly used in the USA.

The most recent survey of child-care arrangements of working
mothers with pre-school children shows that more than half depend
primarily on care by family members or other relatives; 15 per cent
use nursery schools or day care centres, 6 per cent hire a sitter who
comes into the home, and 22 per cent send their children to the home
of a non-relative (US Bureau of the Census, 1983). Day-care homes
are thus an important source of out-of-home care. In some states they
are licensed if they provide care for several children, but in the
mid-1970s it was estimated that no more than 6 per cent were
state-licensed (Browne, 1984). The majority of day-care centres are
run by non-profit organisations including churches and communities;
about 40 per cent are run for profit (National Center for Education
Statistics, 1980). Some employers run day-care centres, but less than
1 per cent of mothers with pre-school children report using centres at
their place of work. Two-thirds of nursery schools are run by private,
but not necessarily profit-making organisations; in addition some
school districts run pre-primary nursery schools.

These estimates of the use of group care may be too low because
the survey was undertaken in June when some nursery schools are
not in operation. In addition some women may think of nursery
schools as educational programmes rather than arrangements for
child-care. Surveys that ask questions about children's school attendance give substantially higher figures for nursery school attendance
by children of working mothers (National Center for Education
Statistics, 1980). Although no strictly comparable figures are available before the 1970s, it does seem probable that the use of out-of-
home care has been gradually increasing.

The National Union of Teachers (NUT) in Britain reviewed the
history of nursery provision in NUT (1973) since 1900. Nursery-
school children aged 3–5 were pushed out of the publicly provided
education system as that system grew, up to 1944. Large classes and
insufficient teachers meant that the 3–5s were gradually displaced.
The major education acts and reports – for example, the 1944
Education Act and the 1964 Plowden Report – have all rec-
ommended that nursery education be expanded, but no funds have
been forthcoming. The NUT (1973) provided figures up to 1970 of the
number of 'maintained' and 'aided and maintained' nursery schools
in Britain. For example, in 1938 103 schools existed, taking in 5666
children; in 1970 482 schools took in 16 138 children full-time and

8493 part-time. Since there is private nursery provision this is far from being the complete picture. The NUT (1973) also cited the figures for hospital nurseries in 1966 as 26 and factory crèches as 79. Play-groups have undergone considerable growth but these do not provide child-care provision for working mothers on the whole. In Britain, nursery provision is argued to be quite inadequate and prohibitively expensive for many families (Bone, 1977; EOC, 1978; NUT, 1973). Some local authorities have provided assistance and subsidies to nurseries but there is considerable variation across the country.

In the USA federal and state governments were first involved in the provision of child care during the depression of the 1930s when nursery schools were funded to provide jobs for unemployed teachers and child care for children from families of the unemployed. During the Second World War the Lanham Act provided matching federal funds to states to provide day-care centres for women employed in defence industries (Zigler and Goodman, 1982). Funds for these centres were discontinued at the end of the war. Since that time tax deductions or credits, benefiting middle-income families primarily, have been enacted at both federal and state levels, and a number of programmes have been adopted with the objective of helping low-income families to become self-sufficient.

A major difference between Britain and the USA is that since 1954 working parents in the USA have received some tax concessions for expenses incurred for child care. Between 1954 and 1975 child-care costs were a deductible expense in computing the amount of income subject to the federal income tax. The maximum deductible amount in 1975 was $4800 for families with incomes up to $18 000. For incomes beyond $18 000 the deductible amount gradually decreased, and beyond $27 000 no deduction could be taken (US Department of the Treasury, 1975). The amount of subsidy available under this scheme depended on the family's income-tax bracket. Some middle-income families may have covered up to as much as 25 per cent of their child-care costs in lower taxes, but most families probably recovered no more than 20 per cent and lower income families much less.

In 1976 the deduction for child-care expenses was replaced by a tax credit of 20 per cent of total child-care and house-keeping costs with a maximum credit of $400 for one child and $800 for two or more children. However, because the credit is not refundable beyond the amount of tax liability, low or moderate-income families will often owe too small an amount of tax to be able to claim the full credit. Nevertheless, the tax credit probably allows more families to claim some reimbursement than the deduction did. Families with incomes above the level where a deduction could previously be claimed are now able to claim the tax credit. In addition, because of peculiarities of the tax law, many middle- and lower-income families who would have gained nothing from the deduction can benefit from the credit. In 1978 over 3 million families claimed some reimbursement for child-care expenses through the tax credit (Beck, 1982).

The tax credit covers care in day-care centres, nursery schools, day-care homes, and care provided by child-minders. Paid care provided by relatives can be covered unless the relative is the child of the taxpayer and under the age of 19, or is claimed as a dependent by the taxpayer. However, if the care is provided in the home of the child, Social Security taxes must be paid in order to qualify for the credit. The Social Security tax owed by an employer is currently about 7 per cent, and this would reduce the effective amount of the credit. It also appears that child-minders and day-care-home workers are often willing to provide care for less in exchange for not having their earnings reported to the tax authorities. Some families undoubtedly prefer to purchase care from this 'hidden economy' rather than claim the tax credit.

In 1984, twenty-eight of the fifty states provided either a tax credit or a deduction of child-care expenses from income subject to the state's income tax. The twenty-two states which provided no tax relief in this way contain about half of the population of the USA (*All States Tax Guide*, 1984). In the states which do provide tax relief, the rules for eligibility and size of the tax refunds are extremely variable. The majority of states provide very modest benefits; most families in these states would probably get no more than 5 per cent of their child-care expenses covered through state tax rebates (Shaw, 1985). Overall then the combined federal and state tax systems probably reimbursed between 20 and 25 per cent of child-care expenses for many families. Some undoubtedly got less and in some cases could claim no reimbursement because their incomes were too low or because they preferred to purchase child care from the hidden economy. A few who lived in states with generous tax rebates probably received larger subsidies.

For low-income families the most important programme in force during the period covered by our surveys was Title XX of the Social Security Act, enacted in 1974 to provide funds to states for social services, including day care. Within certain guidelines, the states were given the authority to decide the amounts and kinds of services to support. Half the funds spent were to be targeted to families receiving public assistance. At its maximum as many as 800 000 children were being served by the programme (Levine, 1981). However, coverage was very uneven across states. A few states did not elect to take federal funds for such a programme; others used funds entirely for children with special needs or for families on public assistance. Some states paid the entire cost of child care; others offered only a partial subsidy (Winget, 1982).

Another programme for low income families is 'Head Start', a federally funded pre-school programme whose purpose is to prepare underprivileged children for school. The fact that the programme would incidentally be providing free child care was probably not considered especially important. Most Head-Start programmes are only half-day programmes, but a few (a recent estimate is 20 per cent) are full-day programmes. Still, even a half-day programme may allow the mother to work part-time or reduce the number of hours of child care for which she must pay in order to work full-time. In 1977 about 350 000 children were enrolled, but it is estimated that less than 25 per cent of potentially eligible children are actually served by the programme (Levine, 1981; Beck, 1982).

Women raising children alone are eligible for Aid to Families with Dependent Children (AFDC) if their income and assets fall below certain levels determined by the state in which they live. Child-care expenses can be deducted from earned income in calculating the amount of payment under AFDC, thus providing an indirect child-care subsidy. As in the case of Title XX, this programme is funded largely by the federal government, but administered by the states; this method of operation leads to extreme variability in the requirements for eligibility and the amount of assistance provided in different states.

The Work Incentive Program, enacted in 1967, was designed to provide training and assistance in finding jobs for women eligible for AFDC. Child care was provided in order to allow women with pre-school children to participate. Other federally funded job-training programmes have also provided child care at times. However, none of these programmes has been sufficiently well funded to serve many of the families that might have benefited.

Since 1980 federal tax credits have been increased slightly, and tax incentives have been enacted to encourage employers to provide child-care benefits to employees.[1] At the same time many of the programmes for low-income families have been cut back. However, these changes occurred after the period covered by our surveys.

The effects of the tax credits and programmes offering subsidised child-care to some low-income families are difficult to assess. As previously mentioned working mothers in the USA are more likely than their British counterparts to use out-of-home and paid child-care. Probably the partial reimbursement of child-care expenses through the tax system as well as the programmes available to low-income families have permitted some women to work without having to depend on relatives for child care. These schemes may also have made it more feasible for women to consider working full-time rather than part-time.

TAX, BENEFITS AND EMPLOYMENT LEGISLATION

Income tax regulations are very complicated to review in detail. We can point out that Britain and the USA are alike in that tax laws are based on the idea that a family has a husband/father at work and a wife/mother at home. It has been argued that these regulations offer married women some disincentive to being employed relative to men in both countries and are therefore the subject of considerable discussion. Income tax in Britain works on a system of allowances. Tax is paid on earnings when they exceed the total allowances. A married man has traditionally received a much larger allowance than a single person before he is liable to tax. A married woman has her own allowance which has effectively been that of a single person. At many income levels therefore, a married couple, both of whom are working, will pay less tax than a married couple with a similar income and family responsibilities where only the husband is earning. The married woman's allowance could be argued to encourage part-time work up to the tax threshold, especially since the marginal tax rate which applies thereafter is high. It needs to be remembered however that many women who work part-time are working to supplement their husband's income, rather than working to benefit from the tax allowance system.

British workers also have to pay a National Insurance contribution. Until 1975 the threshold for payment was that a worker who worked at least 8 hours per week would pay a flat-rate insurance contribution. One might think that this scheme would act as an incentive to

restrict the hours of work to lie inside the national insurance
threshold except that until 1977 married women could opt out of
paying insurance, and many did so, although employers did not have
this option. Graduated pension contributions have been partially
earnings-related since 1960. Since 1977 in Britain there has been
more of an incentive for women to restrict their hours to fall below
the earnings threshold of the national insurance liability. For example, in 1979 with a threshold of £19, a woman earning £19.50 would
have to pay £1.27 per week insurance contribution, and the employer
would pay roughly double that – £2.63. Over a very small part of our
period have there been some tax incentives for women to want to
work part-time therefore, but there have been more tax incentives
for employers to offer part-time jobs. In Britain, unlike the USA, an
employer does not now pay more national insurance for two part-
time jobs than for one full-time job until they earn the equivalent
joint wage. The period during which Selective Employment Tax
operated between 1966 and 1973 was an exception and this tax was
generally regarded as being a disincentive for employers to employ
part-time workers.

In addition, from the employers' point of view, prior to 1977
part-time employees were not protected by much of the employment
legislation which existed. Since 1977, employment protection has
been extended to part-time workers working 16 hours or more per
week, or for workers with five years of continuous service working 8
hours or more. Over much of our period therefore part-time work in
Britain has not required the same level of fringe-benefit payments
from employers, nor implied the same level of worker security.

The tax treatment of married couples in the USA has changed over
time. In 1948, married couples were allowed to benefit from 'income
splitting'. Under this scheme, a married couple could file a joint
return with the combined income of both partners split in half with
taxes being paid on each half irrespective of who earned it. Under the
progressive tax system, income splitting represented a considerable
tax saving for a couple where one spouse earned most of the taxable
income. As such it acted as a disincentive to married women to work.

Under this system, single taxpayers were paying as much as 40 per
cent more tax than is paid on the joint income of a married couple
where the income is the same. The inequalities of this system were
recognised and Congress lowered the tax schedule for single individuals
in 1969, becoming effective in 1971. Married couples could not use
the singles' schedule. However, this new system was soon seen to

have a 'marriage penalty' since two single people would generally find that their total tax bill was higher after marriage. The closer their earnings to each other, the greater the penalty (Gordon, 1979). In 1981 the tax law was changed again as a result of pressure to eliminate the marriage penalty; 10 per cent of the earnings of the spouse with lower earnings may now be deducted in computing the income subject to tax.

During much of the period we are considering there has either been a disincentive for wives to work, or, if they do work, an incentive for them to earn less than their husbands which we could consider an incentive to work part-time. At least we can say from this comparison between Britain and the USA, that in the personal income tax laws in Britain, there is no particular incentive which is absent from the USA, for women to work part time.

Unlike the situation in Britain, in the USA payroll taxes may tend to discourage employers from offering part-time employment (Eisner, 1978). Social Security and unemployment insurance taxes have been levied on all employees with minor exceptions for very short-term employment. In both cases a ceiling is imposed on the amount of earnings subject to the tax. In 1967 the first $6600 of the earnings of any one employee was subject to the Social Security tax, but after 1970 the ceiling was increased each year and reached $25 900 by 1980. Only the first $6000 paid to an employee was subject to the unemployment insurance tax in 1980. In both cases these ceilings mean that it is cheaper to hire one person whose earnings exceed the ceiling than to hire two part-time people to do the same job and pay both of them less than the ceiling.

For the Social Security tax the ceiling is now so high that few women earn above this level, and even in 1967 only a few professional women workers would have had earnings above the ceiling. However, the great majority of women working full-time earn more than the unemployment insurance ceiling. In 1980 the Social Security tax was about 6 per cent of earnings. The unemployment insurance tax varied from state to state and by the individual employer's record of laying-off workers. The base rate was about 3 per cent, but many employers pay 4 or 5 per cent, and a few must pay at considerably higher rates. Whether these taxes have given employers a positive preference for hiring women as full-time workers is difficult to tell, but at the very least, there has been no incentive to hire part-time workers in the USA.

In summary, the USA is clearly ahead of Britain in the length of time that equal opportunities legislation has been in effect and in its more aggressive enforcement of anti-discrimination laws. The USA has far more extensive policy provision for the expenses incurred in child care and Britain has a statutory maternity-leave scheme. The differences between the two countries in the treatment of child-care expenses and maternity leave may not be as great as would at first be supposed, however. Although some women in the USA receive partial reimbursement of child-care expenses through the income-tax system, the amounts involved are typically small and rarely cover more than 20 per cent of costs. British women have the advantage of maternity-leave provisions, but many women do not meet the requirements for receiving benefits; on the other hand nearly half the young employed women in the United States work for employers who provide either paid or unpaid maternity leave as a fringe benefit. There are differences in the demand-side incentives to offer part-time work in the two countries and part-time jobs are clearly more attractive to employers in Britain than in the USA. In the supply-side tax incentives there are more similarities than differences between British and American women. Our analysis of women's experiences will illustrate the effects of the differing legal framework and economic structures of our two countries.

EXISTING TESTS

Since the Equal Pay Act came into full force in Britain in 1975 there have been several attempts to find out what difference, if any, it has made to women's and men's relative earnings. Studies have found it difficult to assess the impact of the legislation because, at the same time, Britain was operating incomes policies of pay restraint and some of the changes in relative earnings which are visible over the 1970s may well be a result of pay restraint. Some of the incomes policies gave flat-rate pay increases to workers, and these have a tendency to equalise differentials.

In Britain, the figures of women's pay relative to men's were stable until the mid-1970s although by the early 1970s women's pay relative to men's had started to rise for both manual and non-manual workers. At the same time women's employment relative to men's also rose but this increase was mainly confined to the non-manual sector. The ratio of wages of women relative to men for full-time manual workers rose from approximately 62 per cent in 1970 to 72 per cent in 1977 levelling off from then on until 1980. For non-manual workers the ratio of women's to men's full-time wages rose from 52 per cent in 1970 to 63 per cent in 1977 and falling to 61 per cent by 1980 (Tzannatos and Zabalza, 1984).

One study by Chiplin *et al.* (1980) attempted to separate the effects of equal-pay legislation and incomes-policy effects in Britain using two data sources; the Department of Employment 'October enquiry' of earnings and the New Earnings Survey data up to 1976. They used a regression model in which relative male – female earnings were explained by unemployment, a dummy for the impact of legislation, an incremental-time trend and time. Equal pay turned out to be less important than flat-rate incomes policies in improving women's position. Since their analysis stopped at 1976 one could argue that it was too early to see the full impact of the legislation. This same criticism applies to a study by Zabalza and Arrufat (1983) of men's and women's pay from the General Household Survey data of 1975 on married people; they suggested that most of the hourly pay differences between men and women could be attributed to women's loss of work experience. They concluded on this basis that the Equal Pay Act had come close to eliminating sex discrimination in pay.

A study by Tzannatos and Zabalza (1984) of the British New Earnings Survey data examined the changes in relative earnings up to 1980. They also concluded that incomes policies and what they call 'the machinery of pay determination' in Britain in the 1970s had an important effect on relative earnings and on the implementation of the Equal Pay Act. Since women's earnings relative to men's continued to remain high after the end of incomes policies, however, they were inclined to think that pay policies were not the whole story. Their analysis suggested that changes in relative pay were mainly caused by changes in pay within industrial and occupational groups and not by a redistribution of women into higher-paying occupations or industries.

A study of 1977 graduates by Dolton and Makepeace (1984) found that there was evidence consistent with sex discrimination even after the Equal Pay Act had been implemented. A comparison of women's and men's earnings from the MRC National Survey of Health and Development of the 1946 Birth Cohort in 1972 and again in 1977 reached a similar conclusion (Joshi and Newell, 1985).

One other study of the effect of the equal-pay legislation in Britain has examined the employment rather than the earnings effects (Pike, 1984). One might expect that equalisation of pay between men and women might reduce women's employment opportunities relative to those of men. One early study, by Glucklich *et al.* (1978) of the implementation of the equal-pay legislation by a sample of British companies, did find evidence that some women's jobs were reclassified so as not to be comparable to men's over the period 1970–5 before the act came into full effect. Tzannotos and Zabalza (1984) suggested that the employment effects were beneficial to women overall. Pike's (1984) analysis of the employment effects of the legislation using data from a Department of Employment Survey of Manual Workers in Manufacturing found that women's relative full-time employment did decline substantially in the period coinciding with the implementation of equal pay. Part-time female employment expanded in manufacturing however and Pike suggests that changes in employment protection legislation, plus the implementation of equal pay may have favoured women's part-time employment in Britain.

Studies of the effects of equal pay and sex legislation in Britain are inconclusive. The evidence does suggest that the legislation has had an impact but that it has not eliminated sex discrimination in pay. The precise effects of this legislation on women's earnings and employment are more debatable. Institutionally based studies like that of Glucklich *et al.* (1978) direct our attention to other changes which might have been occurring in Britain and which might have served to reinforce or even extend labour-market segmentation. Few of these earnings studies have been able to undertake their analysis in the context of sexually segmented labour markets. We hope that our analysis of women's life-cycle occupational changes will provide a better framework for future analyses of the effects of legislation in each country.

The earliest studies of the effects of the Equal Employment Opportunities (EEO) legislation and the Federal Contract Compliance (FCC) efforts in the USA found no effect or in some cases a negative effect on women's employment (Goldstein and Smith, 1976; Heckman and Wolpin, 1976). However, these studies covered the period before 1972 when most enforcement efforts were focused on racial discrimination. Both studies found increased employment of black males in industries in which federal contracts were common. In a study limited to manufacturing industries for the period 1966–78, Leonard (1984) also found that the frequency of Title VII litigation in a given industry had no effect on white women's employment, but increased the employment of black men and women.

Later studies have found positive, though generally not very large, effects of these programmes on women's employment, earnings, and occupational advancement. In a study using the records of companies reporting to the EEOC in 1974 and 1980, Leonard examined the effects of holding federal contracts, of having actual contract reviews, and of various aspects of the review process on women's share of the firm's employment. He found that the employment of women increased faster in firms with federal contracts and that actual review increased the employment of black women, but not of white women (Leonard, 1984a). Leonard speculated that at a time when white female employment was increasing rapidly in the entire economy, a review process that demanded only that the firm's employment of women should increase would not necessarily ensure that the firm would increase its female staff at a faster rate than other firms. However, firms that set high goals for employing women under the review process did increase their hiring to a greater extent than other firms even though actual goals were seldom met (Leonard, 1985). In addition, firms that were growing rapidly were more likely to meet their goals; this finding points up the importance of an expanding economy for the realisation of increased opportunities for women.

Whether EEO legislation and affirmative action programmes have or have not increased the total number of women employed in the USA, it is important to determine whether these programmes have had a positive impact on earnings and the quality of jobs women hold. In a study of male and female earnings differences, Beller (1979) found no effect for the FCC programme but concluded that the Title VII programme had reduced the male – female earnings differential by about 7 percentage points between 1967 and 1974. Although government statistics show no narrowing of the actual differential during this period, Beller's results allowed for the fact that the increased entry of inexperienced women into the labour force would otherwise have depressed women's earnings. Underscoring the importance of economic conditions, another study by Beller (1980) showed that women's potential gains from the EEO legislation were retarded by the recession of the mid-1970s.

Beller's results have been questioned on the grounds that the variables she used to measure the impact of the EEO programmes are not adequate and that the demonstration effects of lawsuits may cause changes in some industries or firms that were not directly affected (Killingsworth, 1979; Wallace, 1979; Sawhill, 1979). This latter criticism poses a problem for all research of the kind being considered here.

Although Beller's results suggest that the EEO legislation has helped to raise women's earnings above levels they would otherwise have attained, the ratio of female to male earnings in the USA (about 0.65 in 1982) is lower than that in many other countries and has been increasing at a slower rate (Freeman, 1984). The female to male earnings ratio increased from 0.62 to 0.65 between 1970 and 1982, but during the same period the ratio in Britain increased from 0.60 to 0.70 according to Freeman's figures. Freeman concludes that countries with centralised wage-bargaining such as Sweden, where female earnings have reached 90 per cent of those of males, have had the best records in improving women's earnings. In contrast EEO laws have had a very modest impact in a country like the USA with decentralised wage-bargaining and a large non-union sector.

As to the effects of EEO legislation on the kinds of occupations women hold, Beller (1982) found that women in states with the EEO suits were more likely to have increased their share of employment in non-traditional jobs. In addition Leonard (1984b) found that women in firms with federal contracts experienced a greater increase in occupational status between 1974 and 1980 than women working in firms not subject to the FCC programme. However, the difference between contract and non-contract firms, though statistically significant, was not very great. Looking at specific occupations, Leonard found that women's increased employment share in contract firms was to be found largely in professional and managerial jobs. No differences between companies with and without federal contracts were to be found in skilled blue-collar and other occupations. It is important to note that Leonard's results may understate the combined effects of the FCC and EEO programmes because his control group, companies without federal contracts, was also potentially liable to discrimination suits under Title VII of the EEO legislation.

The finding that the largest affirmative action impact has been felt in professional and managerial employment is confirmed by a survey of large companies (Shaeffer and Lynton, 1979). Most of the changes in personnel policies reported by these companies concentrated on recruiting or promoting more women into managerial and professional jobs. Attempts to hire more women in skilled blue-collar jobs were deemed much less successful than attempts to hire women for higher level white-collar occupations. The companies surveyed expressed fairly positive opinions about the effects of affirmative action programmes. Many felt that they had gained access to a larger group of qualified workers and that personnel practices had improved as they looked more carefully at their previous policies.

An indirect indication that the FCC programme has contributed to better jobs for women was found in a study of the effects of the programme on the likelihood that a woman would quit her job in a given year. This study indicated that, after controlling for a number of factors associated with job turnover, women working in industries most involved in federal contract reviews were less likely to quit their jobs than were women in industries with a low incidence of federal contracts and contract reviews (Osterman, 1982). Since other research has shown that job-turnover decreases as salaries and occupational status increase, the lower quit-rates in industries subject to FCC reviews were thought to provide evidence of improved job opportunities for women in those industries.

Although these studies on the effects of antidiscrimination efforts in the USA on women's job opportunities have produced somewhat mixed results, on balance this research suggests that this legislation has improved women's job opportunities at least moderately. In a time of rapid increase in women's labour-force participation, gains in employment that can be attributed to litigation or affirmative action have been difficult to document. Although the gap between men's and women's earnings has narrowed slightly, the role of the legislation is again uncertain. The largest impact has probably been on opening up more managerial and professional jobs for women and producing a climate in which more young women acquire training for these jobs because they perceive that women's opportunities have improved.

THE TWO SURVEYS

The information available from these two surveys permitted a series of direct comparisons between British and American women's experiences. Direct comparisons of this kind are rare. There are some differences between the surveys, however. Most notably the WES collected information in 1980 about British women's past experiences on the basis of their memory recall. The potential inaccuracies of such a method have been checked as far as possible against other information collected in the survey, and the researchers involved were satisfied that the work-history data were of a high quality. The NLS is a genuine longitudinal survey which has interviewed the two cohorts of American women repeatedly since 1967–8. The potential problems for our comparisons which could have arisen from the difference in the two surveys were scrutinised especially in the light of the findings and the conclusion was reached that the findings reflect genuine differences in British and American women's experiences. A full discussion of these problems and the nature of the two surveys can be found in Appendix A.

In order to make direct comparisons between British and American women, two cohorts of British women were drawn out of the WES data to match the American women by age. We will refer to these cohorts from here on as *younger women* or *older women*, the definitions of each being as follows:

younger women were aged 14–24 on 1 January 1968
older women were aged 30–44 in May 1966.

The numbers of women in each group are set out in Table 1.1. The American sample sizes are based on the numbers remaining in the survey by 1980 when the WES survey was undertaken.

TABLE 1.1   *Sample sizes of the two surveys for this analysis*

	Younger	Older
British	1423	1705
American	3509	3538

The American sample contains an oversampling of black Americans which means that in the analysis blacks are weighted by the inverse of their probability of falling into the sample. Other details about the comparisons and the ways in which British and American data were made equivalent are described alongside a discussion of the relevant findings.

PLAN OF THE BOOK

The rest of the book is devoted to a comparison of British and American women's work-history patterns. We focus primarily on women's period of family formation because the American surveys in particular contain most information about this phase of women's experiences. In the next chapter we summarise some of women's working and family-formation experiences before going on in Chapter 3 to focus on the timing of the first return to work and the duration of time spent out of employment before that return. In Chapters 4 and 5 we examine the occupational and industrial transitions which women make over their period of family formation. Finally, in Chapter 6 we draw together the conclusions about the effects of social policies and legislation in our two countries.

NOTE

1. The child care tax deductions to employers were part of the ERTA, the Economic Recovery Tax Act of 1981.

2 Women's Work and Family Responsibilities

WORK PATTERNS

If we look at women's employment at a recent point in time, we see that older British women in their forties and fifties were somewhat more likely to be employed than their American counterparts, but the differences were not large (Table 2.1). Among younger women in their late twenties and early thirties, however, American women were much more likely than British women to be employed; the difference between employment rates in the two countries was about 20 percentage points for women in their late twenties and nearly 10 percentage points for women in their early thirties.

When we look at the employment histories of women in the two countries over the past twelve years, we see that older British women had also worked less than their American counterparts when they were in their early thirties, but during their forties British women began to be employed at a higher rate than American women (Figures 2.1 and 2.2).[1] The work experiences of the British women's cohort appears to follow a U-shaped course with a high rate of

TABLE 2.1 *Percentage of women employed at dates of NLS interviews*[a]

Age	British[b]	American
26–30	45.3	65.0
31–5	54.5	63.5
43–7	67.7	63.1
48–52	61.0	57.9
53–6	53.1	50.1

[a] January–March 1980 for young women
April–June 1979 for older women
[b] Younger British women, February 1980
Older British women, May 1979

22

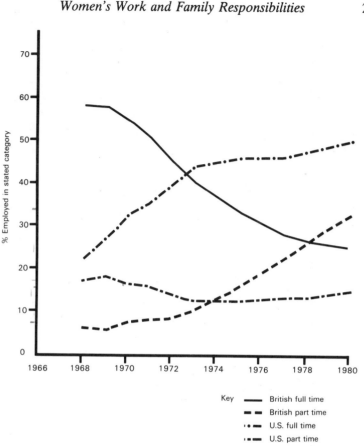

FIGÚRE 2.1   *Employment rates of younger women*

employment from school-leaving age until about 20. After marriage or childbearing a large decline in employment occurs, but by their late twenties or early thirties more women begin working until another high employment plateau is reached in the forties.

A similar U-shaped pattern prevailed among American women in earlier years, but among younger American women a different pattern appears to be evolving. After the usual school-leaving age of 18, employment increases rapidly. For women born between 1944 and 1948, a small decline occurred during their twenties, making a very shallow U-shaped employment profile, but for women born between

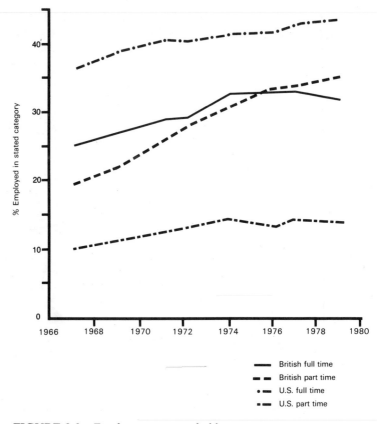

FIGURE 2.2   *Employment rates of older women*

1949 and 1953, employment continued to increase throughout their
twenties. Although it is possible that these women will have a period
of declining employment during their thirties, a trend toward very
early returning to work after childbearing which we describe in
Chapter 3 makes this outcome appear unlikely.

A striking difference between British and American women appears in the hours they work per week as shown in Table 2.2. If we
examine the distinction between full-time and part-time work using
the British definition of part-time (30 hours or less) we find that
British women work part-time far more than US women. Of the
younger women, approximately 57 per cent of British women but

only 23 per cent of American women were working part-time in 1980. For the older women the proportions working part-time were 50 per cent for the British and 25 per cent for the American women.[2] A breakdown of working status by age (the figures are not shown here) revealed that at younger ages few British women worked part-time, but in recent years part-time workers have exceeded full-time workers from the mid-twenties onward. On the other hand, full-time work is much more common than part-time work among American women of all ages.

A breakdown of the usual hours worked by women employed at the time of the 1980 surveys (Table 2.2) shows that the part-time versus full-time distinction conceals further differences in hours worked. About 50 per cent of British part-time workers worked between 20 and 30 hours per week whereas 60 per cent or more of American part-time workers fell in this category. Similarly, about 40 per cent of British full-time workers worked 40 or more hours a week compared with about 80 per cent of American full-time workers. Thus employment rates conceal very large differences in the numbers of hours spent in paid employment in the two countries. Had we adopted the US definition of part-time work (less than 35 hours) however, the differences between Britain and the USA would still be great. The clusterings in the USA and Britain are very similar with most women working part-time for 20–30 hours and full-time for over 35 hours per week.

TABLE 2.2 *Usual hours worked per week (excludes overtime)[a]*
(Percentages)

Hours per week	Younger Women		Older Women	
	British	American	British	American
0–9	9.6	3.5	6.6	2.3
10–19	21.4	5.9	16.0	5.8
20–30	25.8	13.6	27.4	16.5
31–4	4.6	2.5	5.7	2.7
35–9	21.5	11.8	22.8	13.1
40+	17.1	62.7	21.5	59.6
Total %	100.0	100.0	100.0	100.0
N=	809	2254	1114	2027

[a] January–March 1980 for younger American women,
April–June 1979 for older American women.

26   *British and American Women at Work*

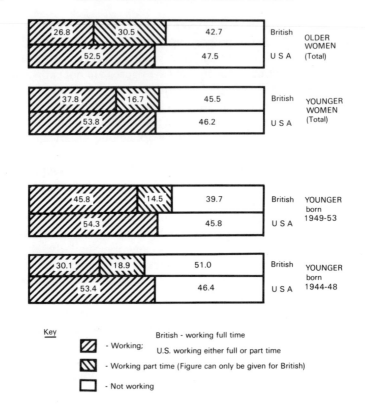

FIGURE 2.3   *Proportion of survey period spent working or not working*

A summary of the total work experience of women in the two countries over the past twelve years is shown in Figure 2.3. Overall, younger women in the two countries were employed for approximately the same percentage of weeks over these years. However, this similarity conceals differences within the group. British women who were in their late twenties in 1980 had worked approximately 60 per cent of the weeks during the twelve-year period, compared with 54 per cent for American women. This difference reflects the much higher rate of employment of British women before age 20 which is not fully offset by higher rates of employment of American women when they reached their mid- to late-twenties as illustrated earlier in Figures 2.1 and 2.2. The situation is reversed for women in their early thirties. British women had been employed for 49 per cent of the previous twelve years while American women had worked for 54 per cent. Older British women (in their forties and fifties in 1980) had been employed for about 57 per cent of the previous thirteen years as compared with 52 per cent of the time for American women. More than half the employment time of older British women was spent in part-time jobs. Although a comparable figure could not be calculated for American women because of data limitations, it appears from the yearly data that probably only 20–25 per cent of American women's employment was part-time during these years.

From the figures we have presented it is obvious that in both countries women's primary responsibilities for raising children strongly influence their employment. Three major work-patterns during the childbearing years can be distinguished: some women do not return to paid employment until childbearing is completed, some work at least part of the time between the first and last birth, and others never return. Among older British women who had children, by far the most common work-pattern was to remain at home from the time the first child was born until childbearing was completed (Table 2.3). On the other hand, older American women were almost

TABLE 2.3   *Work-patterns after childbirth up to 1980 for all women with children by 1980[a] (shown as per cent)*

Work-pattern	Younger women		Older women	
	British	American	British	American
Never returned since first child	27.4	16.9	11.3	7.9
Returned after completing all births[b]	40.3	37.0	59.5	45.9
Worked between births	31.5	46.1	28.4	44.8
Never worked	0.8	0.0	0.8	1.4
Total per cent	100.0	100.0	100.0	100.0
Sample Size	1191	2247	1492	3036

[a]   1979 for older US women

[b]   Includes women who have had only one birth and have returned to work since this birth

as likely to work between births as to wait until their families were completed before returning to work.

Although returning after completing all births is still the most common pattern among younger British women, a trend toward working between births appears to be developing in Britain as well as the USA. Since the childbearing period is not yet completed for many younger women, comparisons between the two countries and between the younger and older cohorts must be tentative. We have counted women with only one birth as returning after all births; if they have another birth, these women will then be counted as working between births. Therefore, among younger women, this latter category can be expected to increase in the future. Even if the percentage who return after completing all births also increases, as those who have not yet had a birth or not yet returned to work enter this category, it appears probable that by the time younger British women reach their forties or fifties, they will be more likely than their older counterparts to have worked between births. Among younger American women, returning to work between births has already become the most common work-pattern, and by the end of their childbearing years a substantial majority of young American women will probably have followed this pattern.

OCCUPATION AND INDUSTRY OF EMPLOYMENT

Although women in both countries are heavily concentrated in such stereotypically female occupations as clerical work, differences in occupational distributions can also be observed from our data. We were able to reclassify US women's occupations using the twelve WES categories to make them directly comparable.[3] American women are somewhat more likely to be employed as professionals or teachers and about twice as likely to be employed in the intermediate non-manual category (Table 2.4). This latter difference may be because American women have found increasing employment in management positions in recent years, sometimes as a result of sex discrimination suits brought against large employers as described in Chapter 1. Although clerical work is the largest occupational category for women in both countries, American women are more likely to be clerical workers than their British counterparts. However, the difference between the two countries in clerical employment is smaller among younger than among older women. British women are

TABLE 2.4 *Occupation of current or most recent job for all women employed in the past 12 months, 1980[a] (shown as per cent)*

Most recent occupation	Younger women		Older women	
	British	American	British	American
Professional	1.0	1.8	0.3	0.9
Teacher	7.4	9.2	5.3	7.8
Nurse	8.4	9.2	5.8	5.8
Intermediate non-manual	6.0	10.9	5.4	10.8
Clerical	27.3	32.8	23.8	34.2
Sales	8.3	5.5	11.1	6.2
Skilled	5.7	8.4	5.7	7.3
Child care	3.1	1.0	1.9	0.7
Semi-skilled factory	9.7	8.8	13.6	10.5
Semi-skilled domestic	9.7	6.2	11.6	8.2
Other semi-skilled	3.9	4.7	3.3	5.2
Unskilled	9.0	1.5	11.8	2.4
Total	100.0	100.0	100.0	100.0
Sample size	927	2594	1202	2238

[a] 1979 data for older American women

somewhat less likely to be employed as skilled workers and somewhat more likely to be employed in semi-skilled factory work as well as in sales, child care, semi-skilled domestic, and unskilled work.

Overall, the occupational distributions of women workers in the two countries exhibit similarities as well as differences. Except for clerical, intermediate non-manual, and unskilled jobs, the difference in employment by occupation never exceeds 5 percentage points. Nevertheless, American women are somewhat more likely to work in the better-paying occupations and British women in the lower-paying occupations. We will discuss possible reasons for these differences at a later point.

The importance of the service sector as a source of employment for women in both Britain and the USA is shown in Table 2.5. Within this sector, professional and scientific services account for about half of the total in both countries. Among other service industries British women are more concentrated in miscellaneous services and American women

TABLE 2.5 *Industry of current or most recent occupation for all women employed in past 12 months, 1980[a] (shown as percentage)*

Most recent industry	Younger women		Older women	
	British	American	British	American
Manufacturing	18.6	15.8	24.1	17.7
Primary production	2.5	1.6	1.7	2.8
Distribution	15.0	17.3	18.5	19.1
Professional, scientific services	29.2	35.0	29.4	33.3
Insurance and public sector	13.2	16.0	8.8	13.9
Miscellaneous services	21.5	14.2	17.4	13.1
Total services	63.9	65.2	55.6	60.3
Total	100.0	100.0	100.0	100.0
Sample Size	926	2601	1203	2236

[a] 1979 data for older American women.

in insurance and public sector jobs. About 25 per cent of older British women are employed in manufacturing compared with 18 per cent of American women, but fewer young British women work in manufacturing, and the difference between the countries is much smaller for this age group. Distribution provides similar percentages of employment in the two countries.

FAMILY COMPOSITION

Differences in family composition of women in the two countries may explain part of the difference observed in employment patterns. Because of the higher divorce rate in the USA, American women are less likely to be married than are British women of the same age (Table 2.6). Younger American women are also more likely than their British counterparts to have remained single. As a result, 86 per cent of younger British women were currently married in 1980 while the corresponding figure for American women was only 72 per cent. These differences undoubtedly contribute to American women's

TABLE 2.6 *Marital status in mid–1980[a] (percentage in each status category)*

| | Younger women | | Older women | |
	British	American	British	American
Single	6.4	12.9	5.1	3.9
Married[b]	86.4	71.8	82.1	76.8
Widowed, divorced, or separated	7.2	15.2	12.8	19.3
Total %	100.0	100.0	100.0	100.0
N =	1423	3509	1705	3531

[a] 1979 for older American women.
[b] Includes cohabiting in British data, in American data includes those who report themselves to be married.

higher rate of employment and full-time working in their twenties and thirties.

Differences in numbers of children may also explain part of the British – American differentials. In 1980 25 per cent of American women in the age range 26–35 were childless while only 15 per cent of British women in this age-range had no children (Table 2.7). The larger percentage of childless women together with the larger percentage of divorced women with children in the USA undoubtedly accounts for part of the 15-percentage point difference in employment rates between the two countries.

Among older women, the differences in employment cannot be so readily attributed to differences in family responsibilities. Older American women have had about three children on average, while British women have had 2.4 children on average. Older British women are indeed slightly more likely to be employed, but in spite of their smaller families British women have much lower rates of full-time employment than have their American counterparts.

The mean ages of these women at their first birth are displayed in Table 2.8. Both older and younger cohorts exhibit the trend towards earlier childbirth, as do both countries. British women have a slightly higher average age at first birth than American women. It is possible, however, that the trend could start to be reversed when childless women in these cohorts in the two countries give birth. The differences between British and American women in respect of their age at

TABLE 2.7 *Percentages with number of children in 1980*[a]

Number of children	Younger women		Older women	
	British	American	British	American
0	15.3	25.2	11.2	10.3
1	20.4	20.7	18.3	9.1
2	40.7	31.5	31.4	22.6
3	17.5	14.4	19.6	21.4
4	4.3	5.6	9.9	15.5
5	1.1	1.4	4.6	8.8
6 +	0.7	1.2	4.9	12.3
Total %	100.0	100.0	100.0	100.0
Mean	1.8	1.6	2.4	3.0
N =	1423	3424	1705	3501

[a] 1979 for older American women

TABLE 2.8 *Mean age of women at first birth*

Cohorts born	Mean age			
	Younger women		Older women	
	British	American	British	American
1922–26			25.2	23.5
1926–31			24.9	23.3
1931–36			24.7	22.2
1944–48	24.0	23.8		
1949–53	22.9	21.9		
Mean of total	23.5	22.7	24.9	23.0

first childbirth are not sufficient to explain any of the differences in their employment patterns. Given that on average, American women leave school later than British women, these figures do mean that British women will have spent longer than American women in employment before childbirth.

EDUCATION

The education and job-related skills of women in the two countries cannot be easily compared because of the great differences in the two educational systems. In Britain, school attendance is compulsory only until 16, and for some of the older women in this sample the school-leaving age would have been 15 or even 14 years old. In the United States school attendance is required until age 16 to 18 depending on state law, but these laws are often loosely enforced as the leaving age is approached and may be waived for pregnancy or other causes. Furthermore, the amount of education represented by a US high school diploma varies tremendously. In some schools students who are functionally illiterate may graduate if they stay in school long enough; other schools offer a thorough preparation for university and maintain academic and vocational requirements for graduation for those who will not obtain further education. Beyond high school, many vocational skills such as specialised clerical skills, nursing and computer programming are taught in two-year colleges. More advanced training in the two last-named areas are also offered at four-year colleges and universities.

In Britain the largest proportion for each age group left school with no educational qualifications; this was 67.5 per cent of the older women. Only very small proportions of each age group had A-level or higher qualification. If we take a British 0-level pass to be approximately equivalent to a US high-school certificate then the comparisons suggest that American women have more education than their British counterparts (see Table 2.9 and Table 2.10).

TABLE 2.9 *Highest qualification obtained by British women by the end of their formal education.*

	Percentage reaching various qualification levels	
	Younger women	*Older women*
None	43.1	67.5
CSE (not grade 1) clerical or trade apprentice	15.0	10.4
O level (CSE grade 1) City & Guilds	19.3	10.3
A level or above (includes degree)	17.3	10.0
Degrees (+ HNC/D)	5.3	1.8
Total %	100.0	100.0
N =	1423	1705

TABLE 2.10   *Highest level of education obtained by American women by 1980 (1979 for older women)*

	Younger women %	Older women %
Less than high school	16.3	33.7
High school graduate	43.3	45.5
Attended college, no degree	14.5	8.2
Attended college, two-year degree	5.2	2.3
Attended college, bachelor's degree (college graduate)	15.9	7.7
Received M.A., Ph. D., M.D., or Doctor of Law degree	4.9	2.6
Total	100.0	100.0
N	3446	3511
Missing	57	27

In both Britain and the USA, younger women have obtained considerably more education than their older counterparts. About 33 per cent of older Americans had not completed high school, compared with only 16 per cent of younger women (Table 2.10). At present about 40 per cent of young women in the USA have attended college or university and about 20 per cent are graduates of four-year colleges or universities or have higher degrees. Only 5 per cent of younger British women had a degree. The majority of the young American women with advanced degrees are teachers, librarians, and social workers, but increases have also occurred in the percentage of women in medicine, law, and other non-traditional fields such as business administration.

ATTITUDES TOWARD WOMEN'S ROLES

Attitudes toward women's family and labour market roles have been found to affect their propensity to work outside the home (Waite, 1979; Shapiro and Shaw, 1983) and to re-enter the labour force after an absence (Shaw, 1983a). In addition, work experience appears to cause attitudes toward employment to become more favourable (Macke, Hudis and Larrick, 1978; Statham and Rhoton, 1983).

Therefore it would be interesting to compare attitudes toward women's roles in the two countries. Both the WES and NLS asked a number of attitudinal questions, but the content and wording of the questions were different, making exact cross-national comparisons difficult. In one case, however, the questions were close enough to make a comparison of responses feasible. In the WES, women were asked whether they agreed with the statement, 'a woman's place is in the home'. In the NLS, the statement was 'a woman's place is in the home and not in the office or shop'. Five response categories were used in both surveys, but since they did not use the same wording, the two levels of agreement and disagreement have been combined.

As Table 2.11 shows, within each of the age cohorts about the same percentage of British and American women agreed that a woman's place is in the home. A smaller percentage of British women disagreed with the statement, but this may have been because of the alternative given in the middle category, which was a neutral 'neither agree nor disagree' in the WES, but limited to 'undecided' in the USA. It may also be the case that the addition of 'and not in the office or shop' would be likely to make for more disagreement because it implies that a woman should not work outside the home at all, whereas without this phrase the statement suggests that a woman's primary place is in the home, but does not exclude some outside employment. While these differences in wording make conclusions tentative, it appears that American women might be slightly more opposed to confining women to traditional roles, but that the sentiment in favour of traditional roles is equally weak in the two countries.

TABLE 2.11   *Response to the statement 'A woman's place is in the home'*[a]

	Younger women		Older Women	
	British %	American %	British %	American %
Agree	20.4	19.0	33.5	32.0
Neither agree nor disagree[b]	19.7	1.9	20.5	4.2
Disagree	59.8	79.1	46.0	63.9
Total	100.0	100.0	100.0	100.0
N	1400	3415	1670	3472

[a] NLS question added the phrase 'and not in the office or shop'.
[b] NLS category was 'undecided'.

TABLE 2.12　*Percentage of working women using specified kind of child care for pre-school children[a]*
(Multiple coding of kinds of care)

Type of provisions used	Younger women		Older women	
	British	American	British	American
Works at home (no external care)	8.2	–[b]	11.1	–[b]
Takes children to work	3.1	5.7	1.6	4.2
Only works in school hours or term	–	3.7	–	4.0
Child cares for self	–	–	–	–
Husband	51.0	16.8	36.0	17.0
Child's older brother or sister	3.1	3.5	3.3	18.7
Other relative	27.6	25.4	41.0	23.9
Person employed in informant's home	4.1	9.4	1.6	12.6
Child-minder, friend or neighbour	21.4	27.2	16.3	15.0
Day nursery, crèche, social services, etc.	6.1	2.6	3.3	0.6
Private nursery, play group, etc.	5.1	14.2	3.3	8.2
Other	–	4.2	–	6.9
Total	129.7[c]	112.7[c]	117.5[c]	111.1[c]
Sample size	98	644	61	45

[a]　Asked in 1978 for American younger women; 1977 for American older women.
[b]　Not asked in USA; included in 'other'.
[c]　Total percentages in excess of 100 because some are using more than one kind of provision.

CHILD-CARE PROVISIONS

Arrangements made by working women for the care of their pre-school children are shown in Table 2.12. The most striking difference between the two countries is the role that husbands play; in Great Britain care by husbands is the most common kind of care, involving 50 per cent of the households of young working women and over 33 per cent of the households of older working women. In contrast, only about 16 per cent of American husbands care for pre-school children while their wives are at work. Care provided by other relatives is also somewhat more common in Britain, except that older brothers and sisters provide considerable child care for older American women workers. American women are more likely than their British counterparts to hire someone to come into the home or to send the child to a private nursery school or play group. Overall, slightly over 50 per cent of American working women depend at least partly on nursery schools, child-minders, or other care provided by non-relatives; the corresponding figure for British women is about 33 per cent. These differences in child-care arrangements may be due in part to the differing hours of work in the two countries. Husbands can perhaps provide child care during their wives' part-time employment, but for women who work full-time other child-care arrangements will usually be required. Women who work full-time are also more likely than part-time workers to earn enough to pay for child-care.

Differences between child-care arrangements in the two countries persist after children enter school (Table 2.13). Although the British husband's role in child care is reduced when children reach school age, 25–33 per cent of husbands still provide care for school-age children while the mother works. Within both countries there are large differences in child-care arrangements based on the ages of the children. School-age children of younger mothers are themselves likely to be quite young whereas those of older mothers are more likely to be nearly grown. Among younger mothers, American women are more likely to ask older children or other relatives rather than husbands to take care of children after school hours, but in both countries some kind of family-related care is most commonly used. In Great Britain, very little extra-familial care is used at this stage, but in the USA about 25 per cent of families of young school-age children still depend at least partly on paid child-care. Even private nursery schools and play groups continue to provide care; increasingly some of these schools accept young schoolchildren for the few hours between the end of the school day and the mother's return from work.

As children grow older they are increasingly likely to care for themselves. In the USA, 50 per cent of the school-age children of older women take care of themselves as compared with about 25 per cent of British school children. Perhaps because of the larger families of older American women, older brothers or sisters are more likely to care for school-age children in the USA, but other relatives more

TABLE 2.13   *Percentage of working women using specific kind of child care for school-age children[a]*

Type of provisions used	Younger women		Older women	
	British	American	British	American
Works at home (no external care)	6.4	_[b]	7.4	_[b]
Takes children to work	4.0	2.6	5.0	3.4
Only works in school hours or term	16.4	11.6	14.0	20.7
Child cares for self	20.5	16.7	25.8	51.3
Husband	32.0	13.3	27.4	9.4
Child's older brother or sister	4.7	11.8	5.0	11.8
Other relative	20.5	27.5	14.0	6.8
Person employed in informant's home	1.0	5.6	1.7	0.8
Child-minder, friend or neighbour	6.7	15.5	7.7	1.4
Day nursery, crèche, social services, etc.	–	0.2	–	0.1
Private nursery, play group, etc.	–	4.0	–	0.1
Other	3.4	3.2	3.3	8.3
Total	115.6[c]	112.0[c]	111.3[c]	114.1[c]
Sample size	297	437	299	930

[a]   Asked in 1978 for American younger women, 1977 for American older women.
[b]   Not asked in USA; included in 'other'.
[c]   Total percentages in excess of 100 because some are using more than one type of provision.

commonly care for the children of older British women. Paid care is not common for older school-age children in either country.

It is probably the case that American women's greater dependence on paid child-care is related to the tax relief for child-care expenses in the USA. Not surprisingly in Britain where there is no help with child-care expenses there is far greater dependence on help from (unpaid) husbands and relatives. British women's pattern of working part-time would also appear to be related to the child-care constraints which they face. We will explore these issues more fully in the next chapters as we examine women's 'not-working' time and their occupational mobility across the first break from work for childbirth.

CONCLUSIONS

American women are more likely than British women to be working during the major childbearing years of their twenties and thirties and are much less likely to work part-time than are their British counterparts. Beyond the age of 40, British women are somewhat more likely to be employed, but continue to be less likely to work full-time than American women. Contributing to the differences between younger women in the two countries is the fact that fewer American women have children and that divorce is more common. However, as the greater numbers of American women who return to work between births indicates, American women are also more likely than their British counterparts to be employed when they have pre-school children. The tax relief which American women can obtain for child-care expenses probably facilitates their working at this time. Differences in the timing of the first return to work after childbirth will be discussed in greater detail in the next chapter.

In both countries women are concentrated in stereotypically female occupations such as clerical work, teaching, nursing, sales and services, and few hold professional or skilled manual jobs. American women are more likely to be employed in the non-manual occupations, however, with the largest differences in the intermediate non-manual and clerical categories, and less likely than British women to be employed in semi-skilled factory, domestic or unskilled work. Service industries are the most important source of employment in both countries.

American women are more likely to utilise paid child-care when they are employed, but child care provided by family members is important in both countries. Husbands play a much greater role in caring for both pre-school and school-age children in Britain than in the USA. Husbands' greater involvement in child care is undoubtedly facilitated by the greater amount of part-time employment in Britain, but child care in Britain is obviously more of a constraint on British women's employment than it is on that of American women. We reckon that the tax concessions for child care in the USA are having a powerful impact on women's experiences.

NOTES

1.   The values for these figures are given in Appendix Tables B1 and B2. The figures for the five-yearly birth cohorts are not listed.
2.   In the WES, part-time employment was defined by the respondent except for the job held at the time of the survey. In the NLS, usual hours of work was ascertained at each interview for women who were working at that date or at any time since the previous interview. In the figures for American women, we have defined part-time work as 30 hours per week or less. In a comparison of self-reported part-time employment in the WES with the number of hours worked in the survey week, Martin and Roberts found that about 8 per cent of women who reported working full-time actually worked 30 hours or less, while about 6 per cent who reported working part-time actually worked more than 30 hours (Martin and Roberts, 1984, p. 34). Since the misreporting is evenly balanced, comparing British women's self-reported full- or part-time employment with American women's actual hours should give a reasonably accurate picture of the differences between the two countries.
3.   The reclassifications of US occupations and industries into the WES categories were carried out with the help of the OPCS and full details are available from the authors.

3 Timing of First Return to Work

INTRODUCTION

The timing of the first return to work involves examining the duration of time women spend not working after their first childbirth. As we have seen from the discussion of the birth-sequence patterns some women return to work after their first child, although they may have other children subsequently. Other women delay their return until they have completed their childbirths and some women never return to work although these are a small minority.

Studies of British and American women have started to examine this duration as longitudinal data has become available. This first break from work for childbirth is significant for a number of reasons; it is one of the key areas of change in women's experiences, the duration has been getting shorter and shorter.[1] This duration has been used in the USA as a criterion to distinguish different types of women; the continuous workers who take very little time off work for a childbirth (less than a year) and those who have a more extended period out of work. On the other hand we must remember that the first break for childbirth is not necessarily the only one so that the first return is not necessarily a permanent return to work. In fact as we saw in Chapter 2 these British and American women's data suggest that the pattern of returning to work between births has been on the increase in both countries. The bimodal pattern was first spotted in aggregate economic activity rates.[2] It is likely that a continuum of experiences exists with continuous workers at one end and women wholly committed to domestic work at the other. (Women with children could become continuous workers by taking maternity leave over every childbirth.) The distribution of women's experiences has been moving towards the 'continuous worker' end of this continuum.

The timing of the first return has been given attention also because

41

it would have implications for women's later experiences, in particular their occupational status. As the duration of time spent out of work for childbirth increases, British and American studies suggest that there is a greater likelihood of women experiencing downward occupational mobility. Our results, presented in Chapter 4, support this idea. It does not appear to be the case in the USA however that women's prospects get progressively worse as they spend more time away from employment, since after a certain length of time the relationship stabilises.[3]

These interests are the background against which we wish to analyse the determinants of women's timing of their return to work and this comparison of British and American women enables us to see the size and scope of the different influences in the two countries. Our analysis enables us to make particular comparisons between British and American women. Statutory maternity-leave provisions are not available in the USA in the same way that they are in Britain (although some companies in the USA have their own private maternity provisions). We can see something of the impact of British maternity-leave provisions through these comparisons therefore. One might expect British women to take a shorter time off work than American women because of this provision but the average durations of time out of employment do not confirm this expectation as we shall see. This gives the results added interest.

DEFINITIONS OF THE TIMING OF THE FIRST RETURN

The first return to work after childbirth would seem to be an unequivocal concept but the fact that women can have different patterns of working during family formation means that there are a number of definitions to consider. (The size of these variations in experiences was described in Table 2.3.) We will call the duration of time spent not working between the dates of the first child's birth and the first return to work LENG (see Table 3.1) bearing in mind that it will include the following family formation patterns:

1. Women who return to work after their first child; it is possible that some of these women will go on to have further children and stop work again therefore in the future, but we will not be concerned with these subsequent stoppages.
2. Women who have more than one child before returning to work;

we would obviously expect this duration to be longer than the case of a woman who returns after the first child.

Another duration variable which can be calculated is YAGE, the age of the youngest child at the first return to work after childbirth. This variable will be exactly the same size as LENG in the case of group (1) whose first return is after their first child. When women's first return is after more than one childbirth as in group (2), the age of the youngest child at the first return will be considerably less than the total duration out of work. Both these variables were calculated and it will be interesting to see whether the influences on each one differ significantly from each other.

DISTRIBUTIONS OF TIMING OF THE FIRST RETURN TO WORK

We can examine the distribution of one of the variables outlined earlier for these two samples; that is, LENG, the duration of time not working after the first child until the first return to work. An issue arises in presenting this distribution about whether to include women who have not yet or may never return to work after childbirth. We have resolved this issue by presenting two sets of results; one excludes women who have never returned to work after childbirth by 1980, and the other set includes them. When they are included their not-working time is calculated from the first childbirth until mid-1980. Since the non-returners are a sizeable proportion we would expect the distribution to change when these experiences are eventually complete. It is interesting and informative nonetheless to compare British and American women who have completed their first return to work after childbirth. Several tables of figures for these distributions are presented in the Appendix Tables B3 and B4 and the distributions are displayed in cumulative form here in the text in Figures 3.1 to 3.4.

The British and American distributions are quite different. The mean length of time away from work for older women who had returned at least once after childbirth was 8.5 years in Britain and 7.7 years in the USA. For the younger women the same mean duration was 4.3 years in Britain compared with 1.6 years in the USA. On average, therefore, women in the USA have much quicker returns to work. The major difference in the distributions irrespective of whether we compare the younger or older women is that in the USA many more women return to work during their first year after childbirth. In the older group approximately 25 per cent of the US women returned to work within a year in comparison with approximately 13 per cent of British women. In the younger groups the figures have increased – almost doubled – in both countries, but the gap between them is still very large. Of the younger American women, who have returned to work, approximately 57 per cent had done so during the first year after childbirth whereas in Britain, the equivalent figure was approximately 30 per cent. These differences are reflected in the shapes of the cumulative distribution; the US curves rise at a much faster rate than the British ones since more women in the USA have returned by any given date after their first childbirth. These effects are also clearly visible in the histogram distributions of the same figures in Figure 3.5.

The fact that the younger generation has changed in the same direction in both countries, moving towards swifter returns to work suggests that the process occurring is the same one in both the USA and Britain and maybe the gap between them means that women in the USA are further along the road than British women in becoming continuous workers. Between American and British women the gap is not caused through British women having significantly larger families as Table 2.7 demonstrated. There is an average age difference of twenty years between the younger and older cohorts which might suggest that Britain is twenty years behind the USA but we suspect that this is not a linear process, in which case 'catching-up' could take a shorter time. The process will be constrained of course by child-care provisions.

If we compare the women who have made at least one return to work after childbirth with the group which includes those who have not yet returned, their distributions in both countries are similar to each other but women who have returned have a steeper sloping cumulative curve. The differences are much smaller in the case of the older woman.

The American results confirm the points recorded in other studies that a group of women exists who return very quickly and are almost continuous workers at least over this first break for childbirth; this means that they combine employment and domestic work successfully. There are also those at the other end of the continuum who have a more extended break from work over childbirth although they are becoming fewer and fewer. Women in the first group do not appear to let childbearing affect their work. There appears to be a similar but smaller group of British women who are close to being continuous workers over their first birth and there may well be more in the future.

However, not all women who returned to work in the first year after their first child was born can be regarded as continuous workers. Many undoubtedly worked only temporarily or left their jobs later to have a second child. Whether these women were able to return to work as quickly after a second birth is a question for future research. In a study that examined the work histories of young women whose first child was born between 1968 and 1973, Mott and Shapiro (1982) found that only about 12 per cent of these women worked continuously for the entire five-to-ten-year period after their first birth.

OTHER STUDIES

There have been a number of studies in the USA of women's working activity around the time of the first childbirth. Studies are numerically greater in the USA because more sources of the necessary longitudinal data required for this investigation are available there than in Britain. Whilst these studies have taken an approach to this issue which is different from the one adopted in this analysis, their results are worth summarising. The American studies on the whole have concentrated on women's working activity over the period of family formation, but obviously their conclusions will have implications in the converse about women's not working activity at this time. The studies cited have different interests; nonetheless there are many overlaps in their findings.

Women's education has been found to influence their return to work in such a way that more highly educated women are either more likely to return to work or return sooner; (see American studies, Shaw, 1983; Mott and Shapiro, 1982; Sorensen, 1983; Smith-Lovin and Tickamyer, 1981; Jones and Long, 1980; Applebaum, 1981; and in Britain, Joshi, 1984; and Dex, 1984). The mechanism through which this effect works has been posited to be an economic one. Education along with occupational status are thought to signify a woman's earnings potential, and the higher her earnings potential the more likely it is that she will want to continue working whilst having children.[5]

The family composition in terms of the number of children, their

YOUNGER WOMEN (EXCLUDING NEVER RETURNED)

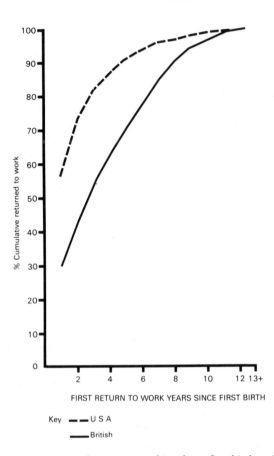

FIGURE 3.1 *Duration of time not working from first birth to first return to work after childbirth – younger women*

ages and whether women returned to work after their first childbirth before having further children have also been found to influence women's re-entry (Shaw, 1983; Mott and Shapiro, 1982; in the USA; and in Britain, Dex, 1984). There are some interesting and perhaps surprising results here, however. Shaw found that for older American women (with at least five years not working) the most common re-entry occurred when the youngest child moved beyond primary grades or into high school, but that women were less likely to re-enter the labour market after their children had left home (the 'empty-nest'

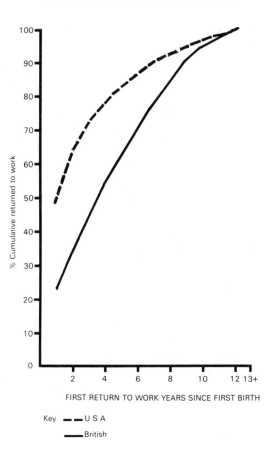

YOUNGER WOMEN (INCLUDING NEVER RETURNED)

FIGURE 3.2   *Duration of time not working from first birth to first return to work after childbirth or until mid-1980 if never returned – younger women*

stage) than they were earlier. Several studies have questioned the idea that women's earlier work and later work experiences are mediated and therefore determined by their fertility behaviour; Mott and Shapiro (1983) suggested that this was not the case for the young American women in their sample as a whole, and that young women's work in the USA is not built around domestic considerations. Also women's early work behaviour did not appear to predict their fertility behaviour or family size. As we have already noted, however, some women, especially in the USA, are continuous workers in

OLDER WOMEN (EXCLUDING NEVER RETURNED)

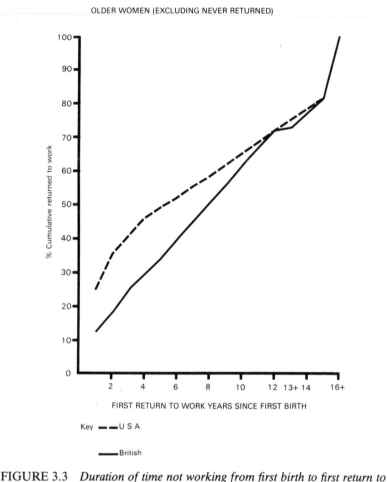

FIGURE 3.3 *Duration of time not working from first birth to first return to work after childbirth – older women*

which case there will be a positive association for them between their pre- and post-childbirth experiences. Economic pressures and less traditional attitudes of women have been found to increase women's likelihood of re-entry (Shaw, 1983, in the USA, and Dex, 1984, in Britain).

Studies have drawn different conclusions about the influence of unemployment rates on women's re-entry decisions. US studies have found that higher unemployment increases women's participation (Wachter, 1972), decreases it (Blau, 1978) and has no effect (Shaw

OLDER WOMEN (INCLUDING NEVER RETURNED)

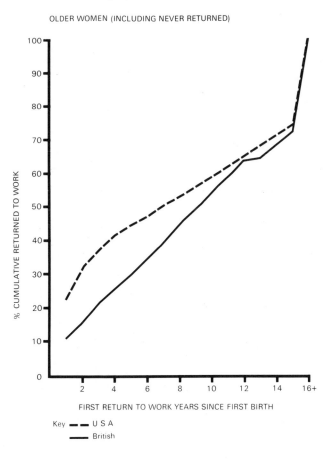

FIGURE 3.4 *Duration of time not working from first birth to first return to work after childbirth or until mid-1980 if never returned – older women*

1983). In Britain, the results in Dex (1984) suggest that higher unemployment delays women's re-entry.

THE TIMING OF THE FIRST RETURN – A MULTIVARIATE ANALYSIS

The longitudinal data available from these two British and American data sources enabled us to calculate the duration of time off work

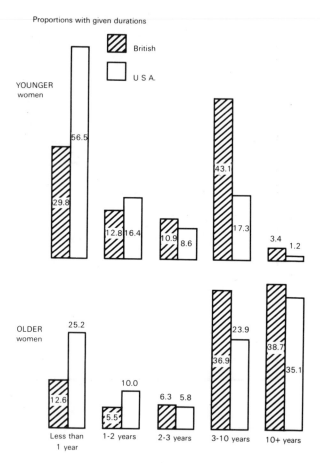

FIGURE 3.5 *Distribution of durations of time not working between first childbirth and first return to work*

over childbirth, but they also provide other valuable longitudinal information about these women's previous experiences. A number of issues and problems arise in constructing a data set to examine this duration. Most of these problems are ones which arise from the longitudinal nature of these data; and they are problems which will undoubtedly be given more consideration in the future. The problems are as follows:

1. This experience of the first break from work for childbirth is unique in a woman's experience and takes place at different points

in time, both chronologically and in the individual woman's life cycle. The data-set constructed pools the information about this unique experience from women of different ages and the resulting data therefore has both cross-sectional and time-series elements. The results need to be interpreted with care, special tests being undertaken of their accuracy.[6]

2. An issue which always arises when using longitudinal data which are incomplete is concerned with what to do with the women who have not yet completed the experience in question. In this case we are interested in the first return to work after childbirth. Some women will have had one or more children but never returned to work; others may be delaying their childbirth and so have no children by the interview. We are including in our sample those women who have had at least one child and who have returned to work after childbirth at least once by 1979–80. We recognise that the biases will be similar in both the British and American results and that comparisons between them will not be impaired.[7] Further research could try applying the proportional-hazards technique to these data.

3. There were some difficulties in making the British and US samples comparable. Precise data on when the younger US women had made their first return to work was usually only available for women who were aged 33 or less in 1980. For this reason two samples of younger women were constructed and the analysis done on both and compared; one group consisted of the whole sample of younger women as far as they were available in the US data and another restricted sample of women below the age of 33 was constructed. An equivalent British sample to match the restricted US women was used alongside the whole British sample of younger women. In the end the multivariate results were not significantly different for these two samples. Only one set of results is reported in the text, the whole sample.

4. The other issues over comparability which arise – for example, occupational classifications – were resolved successfully by reclassifying the American occupations using the British WES occupational categories.[8] Education qualifications are quite different in Britain and the USA so that separate variables were used to capture the effects of education in the two countries. Regression analyses were carried out on the two dependent variables already described, LENG and YAGE, which are both aspects of women's experiences over this period. The two durations were regressed

TABLE 3.1   *Glossary – variable definitions*

LENG	Duration of time from first birth to first return to work to nearest year
YAGE	Duration of time from birth of last child before first return to first return to work, to nearest year – that is, age of youngest child at first return to work, to nearest year.
TREND	Linear time trend attached to year of birth of woman. In older women's sample 1922 = 1; in younger women's sample, 1944 = 1.
PROF	Professional occupation as last job before stopping work for childbirth. Dummy = 1.
TEACH	Teacher occupation as last job before stopping work for childbirth. Dummy variable = 1.
NURS	Nurse occupation as last job before stopping work for childbirth. Dummy = 1.
INTE	Intermediate non-manual occupation as last job before stopping work for childbirth. Dummy = 1.
CLER	Clerical occupation as last job before stopping work for childbirth. Dummy = 1.
SKIL	Skilled occupation as last job before stopping work for childbirth. Dummy = 1.
SEMF	Semi-skilled factory occupation as last job before stopping work for childbirth. Dummy = 1.
QUAL1	Highest qualification reached on leaving school is CSE or clerical or trade apprentice. Dummy = 1 (British sample only).
QUAL2	Highest qualification reached on leaving school is 0-level or CSE (grade 1) or City and Guilds (British sample only). (Having A-level or a degree was very highly correlated with the occupational variables – 'teacher' in particular – and was therefore omitted).
NOTHS	Did not complete high school = 1; High school completion or higher = 0 (American sample only and equivalent to QUAL1).

against the same set of variables and these variables are now described.

Explanatory variables

A full set of variables with their precise definitions is provided in Table 3.1. We can summarise their expected influence here. A set of occupational and educational dummy variables have been included and together these are thought to reflect the opportunity cost of

MATL	Took maternity leave for first child.
WORK	Duration of time working prior to childbirth to nearest year. This can include short breaks of unemployment and full- or part-time jobs.
MTIME	Time between marriage and first birth in years.
HOME	Women's attitude to, 'A woman's place is in the home' 5-point scale; 5 = strongly agree. (As revealed at the 1980 interview).
YCHILD	Woman's attitude to whether women with pre-school children should stay home to look after them. 4-point scale. Women ought not to work = 4 (as revealed at the 1980 interview). Only applies to younger sample.
SCHILD	Women's attitude to whether women with children at school should not work; 4-point scale, women ought not to work = 4 (question as asked at 1980 interview). This variable only applies to older women's sample.
HUSB	Husband's attitude – wife thinks husband prefers her not to work; dummy if wife agrees (as revealed at the 1980 interview).
FAMINC	For the British data this variable is constructed as a proxy for a husband's income measure. A scale constructed using husband's income by age and socio-economic classes, because husband's income had too many missing variables. Faminc = 1 if husband unemployed or wife divorced or widowed before first return to work; Faminc = 5 if husband in professional – managerial job. In the American data husband's actual earnings were available in the year of the woman's return to work in thousands of dollars.
NOLDCH	Number of older children at first return to work – that is number of children − 1.
RACE	Dummy variable = 1 if the woman is black, and zero otherwise. (This variable only applies to the American sample).

women not working; higher occupation and education levels would be expected to have negative coefficients, thus reducing the duration of time not working since their potential earnings will be higher and the opportunity cost of not working higher therefore; these variables also capture human capital effects. Lower level categories would be expected to have the reverse effects. The occupational categories used are those of the WES survey, with US occupations having been reclassified to match the British categories. The WES categories were based on socio-economic groups and therefore have an approximate ranking. Studies by Joshi (1984) and Dex (1984a) were used to modify that ranking in constructing the set of dummy variables used. The base against which other occupational dummy variables are measured is a combination of unskilled and other semi-skilled, domestic, child care, shop assistant occupations which all had the lowest levels of pay in the WES data. Separate British and American education categories have been used; two variables for Britain (QUAL1, QUAL2) and one for the USA (NOTHS). The indicators of education were restricted to these variables since other levels of education were highly correlated with the woman's occupational status. Professional, teacher, nurse and intermediate non-manual occupations capture the effects of both occupation and higher levels of education. We are regarding the completion of a high school certificate in the USA as being roughly equivalent to British O-level passes.

The amount of women's working experience prior to childbirth (WORK) has been included to see how far working experience is cumulative. This variable is an additional indicator of women's earnings potential. Previous studies in Britain and the USA would lead us to expect a positive relationship on past working experience signifying that there is continuity in women's work attachment largely because of human capital effects. The time between marriage and the first birth (MTIME) has been included. This variable is an indicator of the timing of the family formation period, and/or the age of the woman at her first birth. It may further indicate the level of family resources which have been accumulated before childbirth; in which case a longer gap between marriage and the first child could promote a longer duration out of work because financial pressures are not so great. On the other hand this variable could be capturing women who place higher priority on their career or families who place higher priority on consumption, in which case, the woman's time out of work may be shorter as the gap between marriage and childbirth increases. Financial considerations are captured in two variables. A family income variable (FAMINC) has been constructed for the British data based on husband's socio-economic group, and husband's actual earnings are available in the US data.[9]

One variable has been included to indicate women's pattern of family formation; it is the number of older children (NOLDCH) at the first return. Women who have a score on this variable are those who have not returned after their first child and must therefore be considered to be less committed to working than those who did return after their first child. We would expect that the existence of more than one child at a woman's first return must have lengthened her duration of time not working. Whilst this is an obvious effect, the inclusion of this variable does provide some interesting information about the economies of scale of family size.

Several attitudinal variables have been included. One study in the USA (Shaw, 1983) suggested that women's attitude change was the most significant explanation of their considerable higher participation rates over time. We would expect that women with less traditional attitudes would return to work sooner than the women with more traditional attitudes. Traditional attitudes were measured by women's response to the question of whether they thought 'A woman's place is in the home' (HOME). This question was in both the WES and NLS surveys. Also, women in both surveys were asked about their feelings towards women working whilst they have either young pre-school or primary school children (YCHILD, SCHILD). Another attitudinal variable (HUSB) is included in all the regressions; it measures whether the woman thinks her husband approves or disapproves of her working. We would expect that husbands who were thought to disapprove of their wives working would restrict the woman's activity. Most of these attitude variables were responses made by the woman at the interviews and they were not necessarily contemporaneous with the experiences we are considering. We should beware of drawing any definite conclusions from these variables, therefore, since they may well be a product of the experience rather than contributors to it.

A dummy variable for black women (RACE) was included in the US sample only, since the NLS survey has been constructed around black and white populations in the USA whereas this is not the case in the British WES data. (All the US results were weighted accordingly.) A linear time trend (TREND) was also included in each set of regressions to capture the secular change in women's experiences; this has been a reduction in their time out of work because of childbirth.

Whether or not a woman took maternity leave was included in the British set of variables but not in the US set and we would expect that those who took maternity leave would have considerably shorter durations out of work.[10] Women who take maternity leave will be those who return to work after their first child. The extent of this provision varies in length over and above the statutory minimum so it is difficult to predict its precise effect. Given that American women on average spend far less time than British women over their first break for childbirth, it will be interesting to see whether British maternity leave provisions make British women more equivalent to their American counterparts. Several other variables were included in earlier versions of the model but they were omitted from the final version whose results are described below.[11] We can now go on to examine the results of the regressions on the two dependent variables.

Duration of time between first birth and first return – results

A full set of means and standard deviations of the variables for both countries are provided in Appendix Table B5. The ordinary least squares regression results for both older women and the whole sample of younger women are displayed in Table 3.2. We can summarise the overall results as follows: the R^2 values, as a measure of the overall goodness of fit, are fairly similar for both sets of younger women's regressions which suggests that this set of variables together have approximately the same amount of explanatory value in both Britain and the USA. For the older workers, the British model is a slightly worse fit than the US one.

The sign on the trend coefficient (TREND) is as we would expect in all cases; women have been returning to work earlier over time. In Britain the younger women have a larger trend coefficient than the older women which suggests that the process of returning to work sooner after childbirth has been speeding up. Whereas the yearly cohorts of British women born in successive years after 1920 hastened their first return to work by approximately one month for every year's increase in birth cohort, the equivalent change per year's birth cohort for the younger women was an earlier return of 2.5 months. By contrast, American older women had a larger trend coefficient than younger women. Possibly this suggests that the process of returning to work earlier has been slowing down in the USA. The effects of these two opposite cohort effects is that American older women have a larger trend value than older British women, whereas younger British women have the largest coefficient. These results would fit an explanation in which American women were thought to be ahead of British women in their quick returns to work after childbirth but that younger British women have more recently been closing this gap.

There are many similarities between the rest of the British and US

TABLE 3.2 Regression results on duration from first birth to first return, LENG (*t* values in parentheses)

Independent variables	Younger women				Older women			
	British		American		British		American	
TREND	-0.21	(6.8)	-0.12	(6.8)	-0.10	(3.8)	-0.27	(9.5)
PROF	-1.54	(1.4)	-0.53	(1.0)	1.49	(0.4)	-2.44	(1.2)
TEACH	-0.84	(1.9)	-0.26	(1.4)	-0.74	(1.0)	-1.08	(1.8)
NURS	-0.71	(2.0)	-0.52	(2.8)	-0.77	(1.2)	-0.15	(0.2)
INTE	-0.04	(0.1)	-0.06	(0.2)	1.84	(1.6)	-0.40	(0.5)
CLER	0.14	(0.6)	0.14	(1.2)	0.85	(2.5)	0.52	(1.7)
SKIL	-0.34	(1.1)	-0.17	(0.8)	0.47	(1.0)	-0.48	(0.8)
SEMF	-0.10	(0.4)	0.20	(1.3)	-0.06	(0.2)	-0.02	(0.0)
QUAL1	0.34	(1.4)	—		0.14	(0.3)	—	
QUAL2	0.22	(0.9)	—		0.12	(0.3)	—	
NOTHS	—		0.04	(0.3)	—		-0.79	(2.9)
MATL	-1.54	(3.9)	—		-4.17	(4.4)	—	
WORK	-0.05	(1.6)	-0.16	(7.7)	-0.15	(4.5)	-0.16	(4.4)
MTIME	0.00	(0.1)	0.03	(1.4)	0.24	(4.6)	0.14	(2.8)

Continued on page 58

TABLE 3.2 Continued

Independent variables	Younger women				Older women			
	British		American		British		American	
HOME	0.10	(1.7)	0.06	(1.3)	0.36	(4.1)	0.27	(2.5)
YCHILD	-0.03	(0.2)	0.06	(1.5)	—		—	
SCHILD	—		—		0.10	(6.0)	0.21	(2.8)
HUSB	-0.26	(1.2)	0.05	(1.3)	-0.76	(2.5)	0.17	(1.7)
FAMINC	-0.02	(0.4)	0.01	(2.6)	0.34	(3.4)	0.04	(4.3)
NOLDCH	2.98	(26.1)	2.90	(32.5)	2.32	(23.6)	2.79	(42.1)
RACE	—		-0.42	(3.2)	—		-2.64	(6.7)
CONSTANT	3.99	(7.7)	1.64	(7.4)	1.76	(2.1)	4.37	(8.0)
R^2, $\bar{R}^2$	0.57,	0.56	0.52,	0.51	0.42,	0.42	0.51,	0.50
F	56.0		84.7		46.2		132.9	
N	767		1364		1147		2217	

results and some clear generational differences which are also similar in both countries. A large number of variables turn out to be insignificant however, especially in the younger women's cohorts. The most important variable in this regression on the duration of the first birth to the first return is NOLDCH, the number of additional children after the first which precede the first return. In the US results, the race variable (RACE) is also significant and black women make a faster return to work after childbirth than white women. The results are discussed separately below.

Earnings potential effects

The occupational and educational variable results represent the opportunity cost to women of not working, and as such, the results are broadly in line with our expectations and with human capital theory effects. The negative signs on the higher grade occupations (professional, teacher, nurse and intermediate non-manual) for younger and older women in both countries illustrate that women with a higher earnings potential return to work sooner after childbirth. The coefficients are not all significant however and this is particularly true of older women in Britain. We suspect one of the main reasons for the insignificant occupational coefficients in the older women's group is that relatively few older women were in these higher grade occupations. Women have been entering these occupations in larger numbers in Britain and the USA only fairly recently.

Where the higher level occupational coefficients are significant – as in the case of teachers – we see that a previous job in teaching hastens a younger British woman's return to work by approximately 11 months on the average and an older American woman's return by approximately one year. The effects of occupation on the duration of not working are among the largest in absolute size in both the British and US samples so that a woman's occupation appears to be an important determinant of her working behaviour, and possibly more so in Britain than in the USA. Since maternity leave eligibility in Britain is also related to a woman's occupation, these results add weight to the importance of maternity leave for British women's labour-market experiences.

In the lower level and intermediate occupations we find some differences between the groups. A clerical occupation has a significant effect for older women in Britain and the USA and it increases the duration of time not working in both cases by approximately six to eleven months; the shorter duration belongs to US women so we can say that the delaying effect on returns to work of clerical occupations is less in the USA.

Educational variables (QUAL1 and QUAL2) have similar effects to occupational variables in Britain, although few are significant. Women with lower levels of education or no qualifications (QUAL1) and presumably a lower earnings potential delay their return to work. In the USA this effect can be seen for the younger women who leave school without a high school certificate (NOTHS), but not for the older women. Older women with few if any educational qualifications appear to return to work faster after childbirth than those with intermediate levels of education. This result is not what the human capital theory would lead us to predict and it is also a way in which American older women differ from the British older women. (There is a possibility that the US results on the education variable are in fact measuring educational differences between the blacks and whites in the USA.)

Women's previous working experience is mostly a highly significant variable and its effects are in line with human capital theory's expectations. Women with longer working experience prior to childbirth make faster returns to work after childbirth. It is interesting that the size of this effect is almost identical in both Britain and the USA for the older women; for every additional year of work prior to childbirth women's return to work after childbirth is brought forward by approximately one sixth of a year on average. If the experience of work affects women's earnings, then again these results suggest that women are responding to their opportunity cost of not working. Younger British women are something of an exception since their coefficient is much smaller and not significant at the usual levels. It is not clear why British younger women differ, especially when there is such uniformity in the results of the other groups.

Family composition effects

The number of older children at the first return to work is a highly significant variable in all the regressions; it is the most significant in every case and also has the largest sized coefficient. On average, an additional child before the first return delays the woman's return by approximately two to three years; the values are not very different for younger and older women, which might suggest that the spacing between multiple births when women do not work in between births, has not changed very much over the generations in either country.[12] We might conclude that the changes which have occurred in women's employment over the family formation phase in Britain and in the USA are associated with changes in the sequence patterns of childbirth and work, rather than with the spacing between births; that is, from women returning to work between childbirths. Changes in family size could also be part of the explanation.

Attitudinal effects

The results on the attitudinal variables (HOME, Y/SCHILD) confirm our expectations that older women with more traditional attitudes towards women's roles and child-rearing responsibilities spent longer not working over their family formation phase. We must be careful in interpreting these results, however, since women's attitudes were only available at a point in time after their return to work. We cannot say unequivocally therefore that attitudes caused this behaviour. Both attitudinal variables are significant in the older women's samples but not in the younger ones at usual levels of confidence. As we noted earlier from other studies, attitudinal change has been suggested as the most significant single factor explaining changes in US women's working behaviour. The lack of significance of attitudes in these young women's experiences may suggest that there is relatively little variation between younger women's attitudes nowadays in the USA and in Britain. Shapiro and Shaw's (1983) results from the USA provide some support for this conclusion. (The means and standard deviations for these variables in Appendix Table B5 also offer some support for this suggestion.)

The same generational difference can be seen in the husband's attitude variable (HUSB), but the effects differ between the two countries. What women say about their husband's view of their working is only significant in older British women's experiences. The result suggests that women whose husbands prefer them not to work return to work sooner than women whose husbands were not concerned or did not mind them working. Thus rather than husband's traditional attitudes delaying women's return it seems to have the reverse effect, but it may be that husbands' views came as a result of their wives' early return; that is, in response to the woman's work rather than prior to it. In fact this is probably the most likely explanation. Possibly it is not a significant effect in the USA because the organisational changes in the household required if women are to work may be less there than they are in Britain. The fact that more British husbands are involved in child care than is the case in the USA supports this suggestion.

In summary, the attitudinal effects visible in these results are not very great although they may be under-estimated in so far as attitudes are embedded in some of the other variables; for example, it is likely that family income and occupations capture some attitude differences. Attitudinal effects were clearly stronger in the older generations.

Economic circumstances

The higher the family income, as measured by husband's earnings, the longer the duration of not working over childbirth. This effect is clear in the US sample and the size of the effect was greater for the older women than it is in the younger. A study of women in the USA by Shapiro and Shaw (1983) found that the responsiveness of a wife's labour-force participation to her husband's earnings has been declining. In Britain the effect is only clearly significant in the older group of women although the measure is less satisfactory since actual earnings of husbands was unavailable. The British results are similar to those of the USA therefore with younger women's behaviour appearing to be less influenced by their husband's earnings than is older women's behaviour.

Correspondingly there are differential effects between the age cohorts on MTIME, the time gap between marriage and the first birth, which was also considered as having a potentially economic impact. The results for the younger women in both Britain and the USA are insignificant. With older women, the additional time before the first birth delays their return. The effect on older American women is smaller than it is on British women. It could be the case that older women saved up, so to speak, to start a family and having done that, they could then afford to take the time off to look after their children. With the younger women, however, it would seem more likely that those who delay their first childbirth after marriage are those with a stronger motivation to work, a stronger preference for consumption, or for independent earnings which they do not wish to give up at childbirth; either way there is a clear generational difference here in both countries.

Maternity leave

British women who took maternity leave had the expected reduction in their time not working. Of the younger women's sample analysed in this regression, 6.2 per cent took maternity leave at their first childbirth and 4.3 per cent of the older women took maternity leave. In the older age group the effect was the largest, approximately four years reduction in time spent not working, although a smaller proportion of older British women had access to this provision since their family formation phase was prior to the introduction of the statutory provisions. The differences between the actual proportion of older and younger British women taking maternity leave for their first childbirth are less than we might expect. It is likely that the full effect of statutory maternity leave provisions is not manifested even in the younger of these two age groups. Of the older women who did have some maternity leave provisions the effect was very considerable and it hastened the return to work of these women in such a way as to put them considerably ahead of their US equivalents.

In the case of the younger women, more of whom will have had access to maternity leave, although they are still a small minority, the effect was to reduce women's time out of work by approximately one to one-half years. Adjusting the constant term for this effect, other things being equal, still leaves British women with longer durations of not working over the family formation phase than the equivalent US cohort. It is a little ironic that the biggest impact of maternity leave occurs prior to the statutory provisions in Britain although this sample of British women is not an ideal test of the impact of maternity leave provisions since some of the younger women would have begun their family formation prior to the introduction of the statutory provisions in 1975.

It is the case, however, that women in the USA appear to have been spending far less time out of the labour market without statutory maternity leave provisions than the equivalent British women. In 1978, in the NLS survey of young women, 20 per cent reported that their employers provided paid maternity leave; another 25 per cent said that unpaid leave was available. Some of the paid leave is undoubtedly linked to worker-insurance policies. Whilst these figures do not indicate the precise number of US women in the NLS survey benefiting from these provisions they give an approximate indication of the provisions of leave at this time. Whilst paid leave is a minority experience the addition of paid and unpaid leave means that nearly

50 per cent of the younger women in the American sample may have been influenced by this. The very low duration of time spent out of work for childbirth by US women is undoubtedly related to these provisions although it would not appear to be the whole story. Since much of this leave is unpaid anyway these women presumably had a high motivation to return to their jobs. Maternity-leave provisions in Britain still appear to be more extensive than in the USA and the effect on British women, as measured in our results does reduce the large gap between British and American women, but it does not eliminate it. By the time the full effects of the British provisions are felt this gap may well decline further. We can examine the take-up of maternity leave by these British women in a little more detail. The figures in Table 3.3 show the mean durations of the last job before childbirth for women who took maternity leave and those who did not.

TABLE 3.3   *Time spent by British women in last job before childbirth analysed according to whether or not the women took maternity leave at their first childbirth*

British cohorts	Mean in months	
	Took maternity leave	*Did not take maternity leave*
Younger	32	36
Older	57	50

Since the eligibility for maternity leave is related to length of job tenure we might expect those who took maternity leave to have longer job tenure before childbirth than those who did not take it. In fact, this is not clearly the case, on the average, as the figures in Table 3.3 illustrate. The expectation is upheld for the older women although the difference in the mean is only seven months. For the younger women, the results are the reverse of what we might initially expect but we must remember that it is likely to be the youngest in this group of younger women who most benefited from the introduction of statutory provisions; the youngest women will be those whose marriage and childbirth are at an earlier age (as demographic trends show) and this will also be affecting their job tenure prior to childbirth.

There are some occupational differences between women who take or do not take maternity leave, however, as the figures in Table 3.4 for British women illustrate. The differences between their occupations are similar in both age groups. Women who took maternity leave in these samples were far more likely to be teachers or skilled workers and far less likely to be in semi-skilled factory or sales. A large proportion of older women who took maternity leave were in other semi-skilled jobs. These results highlight the unevenness of maternity-leave provisions between occupations and in particular the low level of opportunities or take-up in semi-skilled factory work. This finding has serious implications given that factory work is one of

TABLE 3.4 *Comparison of occupations before childbirth of British women who did or did not take maternity leave for first childbirth*

Occupation of last job before first birth	Younger women		Older women	
	Women who took maternity leave for first birth	Did not take maternity leave (but had children)	Women who took maternity leave for first birth	Did not take maternity leave (but had children)
	%	%	%	%
Professional	–	1	2	–
Teacher	14	5	7	3
Nurse	7	7	2	4
Intermediate non-manual	7	3	7	1
Clerical	36	37	15	30
Sales	7	13	8	12
Skilled	14	8	20	8
Child care	–	1	–	1
Semi-skilled factory	8	20	17	27
Semi-skilled domestic	6	2	5	5
Other semi-skilled	3	3	17	6
Unskilled	–	1	2	2
Total %	100	100	100	100
N =	73	1100	60	1382

the dominant women's occupations. It is not all manual work which has low take-up however since the skilled category covers predominantly manual work occupations. These results stress the importance of women's occupations in influencing their experiences, as we saw earlier.

Before summarising the major similarities, differences and generational effects, we can examine the other regression results.

Age of youngest child at mother's first return to work – results

The same set of variables as in Table 3.1 were included in a regression on a different dependent variable, the age of the youngest child at the first return to work, YAGE. We would not expect the results to vary significantly from those described already but they offer a slightly different perspective on women's behaviour. In the previous regression (LENG) the pattern of women's family-formation experiences was part of the dependent variable – duration of time not working. Here we can separate out more of the sequence pattern effects from effects concerned with the age of the child at a woman's first return to work. The mean and standard deviation of the new dependent variable are included in the list of all variables in Appendix Table B5. The full set of regression coefficients for the age of the youngest child at the first return to work, YAGE, are listed in Table 3.5. The overall fit is much lower in these regressions; R^2 values lie between 0.15 and 0.23 for the British women and 0.15 and 0.20 for the American women. In many other respects, whilst the sizes of the coefficients have altered, and slight changes in significance levels have occurred, their relationship to each other between the generations in one country, and between the two countries has remained fairly stable.

The two consistently most significant results are the trend (TREND) and the number of older children (NOLDCH) variables. The trend indicates that the age of the youngest child at the woman's first return to work has been declining and again younger British women appear to be catching up on American women who return to work sooner after their last (youngest) childbirth. The effect of older children in this case is considerably smaller, as one would expect, but it is still positive; that is, having an older child delays a woman's first return to work after her latest child by six months to one year. The

TABLE 3.5 *Regression results on age of youngest child at first return, YAGE (t values in parentheses)*

Independent variables	Younger women				Older women			
	British		American		British		American	
TREND	-0.20	(6.5)	-0.09	(5.8)	-0.19	(4.4)	-0.20	(8.1)
PROF	-1.57	(1.5)	-0.48	(1.0)	1.60	(0.4)	-1.30	(0.7)
TEACH	-0.68	(1.6)	-0.16	(1.0)	-0.47	(0.6)	-0.35	(0.7)
NURS	-0.49	(1.5)	-0.35	(2.0)	-0.55	(0.9)	-0.08	(1.0)
INTE	0.05	(0.1)	-0.02	(0.1)	1.20	(0.9)	0.02	(0.0)
CLER	0.13	(0.6)	0.17	(1.6)	0.58	(1.7)	0.58	(2.2)
SKIL	-0.63	(2.1)	-0.15	(0.8)	0.09	(0.2)	0.13	(0.2)
SEMF	-0.02	(0.1)	0.22	(1.5)	-0.14	(0.5)	0.13	(0.4)
QUAL1	0.60	(2.5)	—		0.14	(0.4)	—	
QUAL2	0.35	(1.6)	—		0.15	(0.4)	—	
NOTHS	—		0.07	(0.6)	—		-0.57	(2.4)
MATL	-1.53	(4.0)	—		-3.70	(4.1)	—	

Continued on page 68

TABLE 3.5 Continued

Independent variables	Younger women				Older women			
	British		American		British		American	
WORK	-0.07	(2.1)	-0.13	(7.1)	-0.14	(4.4)	-0.12	(3.9)
MTIME	0.02	(0.5)	0.03	(1.4)	0.24	(5.0)	0.14	(3.3)
HOME	0.07	(1.2)	0.03	(0.9)	0.38	(4.4)	0.14	(1.5)
YCHILD	-0.01	(0.1)	0.06	(1.8)	—		—	
SCHILD	—		—		1.01	(5.6)	0.20	(3.2)
HUSB	-0.33	(1.6)	0.07	(2.0)	-0.64	(2.1)	0.09	(1.0)
FAMINC	-0.04	(0.6)	0.01	(1.8)	0.27	(2.8)	0.03	(3.7)
NOLDCH	0.87	(8.2)	0.97	(12.0)	0.55	(5.6)	0.68	(12.1)
RACE	—		-0.38	(3.2)	—		-1.79	(5.3)
CONSTANT	3.98	(8.1)	1.38	(6.9)	1.85	(2.3)	3.57	(7.6)
R^2, $\bar{R}^2$	0.23,	0.21	0.20,	0.19	0.16,	0.15	0.15,	0.14
F	12.6		20.1		11.5		22.0	
N	770		1364		1115		2217	

delaying effect is smaller for older women in both countries than it is for the younger women.

The generational differences in the effects of a woman's attitudes are found again in these results, the traditional attitudes of older women having significant delaying effects on their first return. The effect of husband's attitudes has a clearer and more significant effect here and the difference between Britain and the USA stands out more; British women with husbands who would prefer them not to work returned sooner whereas in the case of American women the reverse is the case. We suspect that different mechanisms are at work here, as mentioned earlier, and that these differences may well be related to the child-care provisions made by families in the two countries.

One other difference between these regression results on the age of the youngest child at the woman's first return and the earlier results on the whole of the first break from work is that the previous working experience (WORK) is significant in the sample of younger British women in these latest results; the effect is negative, as it is for the other groups; more work experience prior to childbirth hastened the return to work.

We can say in conclusion that the age of the youngest child at the first return to work is influenced broadly by the woman's earnings potential, her past working experience, her attitudes if she is older, her family income in most cases, and her family size at the first return, as well as the decreasing trend towards earlier returns to work. These are a mixture of life cycle, family cycle, human capital and general economic supply-side incentives. Maternity leave also considerably reduced the age of the youngest child for British women, but in this case, the effect is the same as that noted in the earlier regressions since it is the same women.

GENERATIONAL CHANGES

We have been able to compare a younger and an older cohort of women in both countries and a number of changes seem to be occurring. In both the USA and Britain younger women have been spending less time over this first break from work for childbirth. The gap is wider between the youngest cohorts with women in the USA having the lowest mean although the change per year in time spent before the first return within the younger cohort is greater for British than for American women. In this sense, the younger British women may be closing the gap between the American and British younger women's experiences.

A number of factors which were important in the older generation have seemingly become less important in the younger age group; older but not younger women may have spent time 'saving up' to have children after they were married; women's attitudes and husband's earnings appear to have less influence on younger than on older women, especially in the USA, and other studies of US women confirm this finding. There was little difference between the generations in the average amount of time spent caring for additional children if the woman did not work between childbirths.

Maternity leave contributed to reducing the time spent out of employment before the first return in Britain, the greatest effect being seen among the older women. It is somewhat ironic that maternity leave had its biggest effect prior to the introduction of statutory provisions but it is less surprising when we see the secular changes which have been occurring anyway. This younger cohort were not of an age to receive the most benefit from the statutory provisions.

CONCLUSIONS

We have found a large number of similarities between British and American women's experiences over their first break for childbirth. The marked trend towards earlier returns to work is common to both countries. The fact that the US women are ahead of British women in this respect may be partly because of their earlier start on equal opportunities legislation. The same set of influences was found to affect them both, albeit to differing degrees; these influences are earnings potential, family composition, family circumstances and attitudes with the addition of race in the USA. Perhaps the most striking difference between British and American women is that women in the USA can be divided more clearly into those who return to work very quickly after their first childbirth and those who spend more time in child-rearing. This is only part of the family formation experiences of many of these women however, although an analysis of the British data in Dex (1984) found that women who worked between their births worked more over their family-formation phase as a whole. In Britain, by comparison, the continuum of experiences is not so weighted to the continuous working end as it is in the USA. In proportionate terms there has been much change recently in Britain between the generations but US women are much further ahead of course in the trend to spend more of their time working over their family formation phase. Younger British women may have been closing this gap.

Maternity-leave provisions in Britain have been reducing the time out of work to a large extent, but they do not close the gap between British and American women, although it may be too early to see the full effects from these British data. A large proportion of younger women in the USA were eligible for some leave at this time, although not many received pay. In addition there are considerable hurdles for women who might want to take maternity leave in Britain. They first have to qualify by working certain hours, in a sizeable firm for a certain period before childbirth. These eligibility conditions severely restrict many women's take-up of maternity leave. We saw earlier, in addition, that the unevenness of maternity leave take-up in Britain is linked to women's occupations; semi-skilled factory work in particular appeared to offer fewer opportunities for maternity leave. Given these restrictions on eligibility for maternity leave in Britain, it could be argued that the results are not so surprising. Maternity leave has not had the size of impact it might if the conditions under which it applied were more favourable. Nonetheless, where women do take maternity leave it has a sizeable effect on their experiences.

Another factor which undoubtedly affects women's working and not-working activity over the period of family formation is the child-care provisions which are available. We were unable to incorporate child-care provision into this regression analysis, since no information about child-care in the past, at the time these events were occurring, was available in our data. We do have information about child-care at the interview and this was described in more detail in Chapter 2. It is worth drawing attention here to the differences we found there since it could be argued that similar differences probably applied in the past at women's first childbirth. We found that relatives, especially husbands, were crucial to the child-care patterns of British women and constituted by far the majority of any provision. These results were thought to be consistent with the greater proportion of British women working in part-time jobs. In contrast, women in the USA relied more on formal and paid child-care which also overlaps with their greater propensity to work full-time and, one suspects, at higher paid jobs. We can note here that there is an overlap between the duration of time not working and the type of child-care used after returning to work. It seems likely that British women will be unable to reduce their duration of not working without parallel developments in (formal) child-care provision. This theme will be developed in more detail in the next chapter. Similarly, in order to be able to pay for the more extensive child-care, women will need to take on better, more highly paid jobs which, from the evidence of the next chapter, are still not widely available to them in Britain. British women appear to be moving in the direction of the American women, but the gap is a wide one.

NOTES

1. See Dex (1984) for documentation of this phenomenon and Corcoran (1979) for an illustration from the USA.
2. A 'bimodal pattern' was identified in Britain by Hakim (1979) from aggregate economic activity rate data.
3. For example, Sorensen (1983).
4. In the younger cohort it was difficult to identify the first return for births which occurred prior to 1967 so that the sample was truncated and the British WES data were adjusted to make them comparable.
5. Economists call this concept the opportunity cost of not working and it is an integral feature of human capital theories.
6. This involves examining cross-sectional year slices through the data and comparing the coefficients from a similar regression run with those obtained by pooling the whole sample. This procedure is explained more fully in Dex (1984). An extensive test was carried out on the WES data of this issue for a different analysis using similar variables with the result that the coefficients were found to be genuine and quite robust. The test was therefore not repeated here.
7. There is some evidence in the USA which suggests that more women are now delaying having their first child to an extent that is reflected in the figures for age at first birth; see Mott (1983). There appears to be a similar trend in Britain although it may not be so pronounced as that in the USA. At any rate, the average ages at first birth in Chapter 2 for these two surveys are not very different so that we feel justified in regarding these American and British samples as being subject to similar biases.
8. The precise details of the reclassification of occupations are available from the authors. The exercise was carried out with the help of the OPCS.
9. See Appendix C for further details.
10. Not all the women in the WES data who recorded very short periods out of employment, particularly when they were older women, took maternity leave. Presumably these women did not qualify for maternity leave.

There is also the possibility that some of the American women had access to a private maternity-leave scheme but we do not have precise details of this possibility.

11. Several other variables were included in earlier versions of this model but they have since been omitted. A dummy variable showing whether a woman had had a divorce was included but the variable was felt to be too imprecise since it was not clear whether she was remarried again by the timing of her first return to work. Also, the effects of being divorced are likely to be mainly financial ones in which case they are already partly captured by the family income variable. Attempts were also made to incorporate the unemployment rate as a time-series measure of demand when the woman was returning to work. It was not clear at what date this variable should be attached however; whether at the beginning of the period out of work, the middle or the end. Since we did not know at what point women were seeking work before they actually returned we could not be sure which levels of demand conditions were appropriate. Attaching the unemployment rate to the year of the woman's return, given that unemployment has been on an upward trend, meant that there was likely to be a (positive) correlation between a longer duration out of employment and high unemployment rates. Several methods of incorporating unemployment rates were tried and the results were found to vary enormously according to the date at which the variable was attached. We decided to omit unemployment in the end because of these differences in the results. Other techniques are needed to explore demand effects on the timing of women's first return to work after childbirth.

12. The precise causality of this variable NOLDCH (the number of older children) is also debatable. One could argue that the longer a woman waits to return to work, the more likely it is that she will have additional children in the meantime. We think that in practice it is difficult to distinguish these two effects since women are likely to make the decisions about working and childbirths fairly concurrently. Some interesting results arise from including this variable.

4 Occupational Mobility

INTRODUCTION

We are interested in examining women's occupational changes around the time of family formation. Women's occupations are important in that they determine to a significant extent the pay which an individual woman receives as well as her employment prospects over the life cycle. Women's occupational changes over their family-formation period are particularly interesting since it is this break from work for childbirth which has been thought to be largely responsible for women's occupational downgrading and for limiting women's occupational advancement. In Britain many women also make a status transition from full-time to part-time work over the family formation phase.

Many other studies have been hindered from examining the nature of women's occupational mobility by having insufficient data on women's work-history experiences. The WES and NLS therefore are valuable longitudinal sources which can fill in some of the gaps left by other analyses.

By comparing British and American women's experiences at this time we hope to begin to answer some of the questions raised by other analyses. If a large part of women's downward occupational mobility in Britain appears to be associated with the part-time jobs which women take after childbirth, is this relationship similar in the USA? If downward occupational mobility over childbirth in the USA is not related to part-time work in the same way or if part-time work in the USA after childbirth does not mean that the woman has experienced downgrading, then an important lesson can be learnt in Britain about women's occupational mobility and the way of changing things. The lack of a relationship between part-time work and downward occupational mobility in the USA would suggest that it is the structure of opportunities for women and the nature of part-time work in Britain which is more responsible for their occupational downward mobility than merely the fact of being part-time.

74

Comparisons between British and American women's experiences of occupational mobility and their distribution through the structure of occupations therefore can teach us important lessons about the way the structure of opportunities influences women's work. Some writers have already suggested links between the structure of occupations and women's experiences, for example, the segmented or dual labour market theories, but these theories are rather crude and they seem to regard women as one homogeneous mass of secondary-sector workers. We are hoping that our analysis will help to construct a clearer picture of the relationship between women's occupational experiences and the structure of employment in Britain and the USA and one which also integrates the important aspect of women's part-time working which is still increasing in Britain.

A counterpart to women's occupational changes is a set of industrial changes which occur simultaneously and we will examine industrial changes in the next chapter. Industrial changes have received far less attention in research on women's work, largely we think because the industrial classification of a woman's job is not highly correlated with rewards in the same sense that occupations are.

This chapter proceeds by sketching the background of the British and American occupational distributions and the changes which have been occurring in them. We also summarise some of the results of other studies of women's occupational mobility in Britain and in the USA before going on to describe the results of our analyses of the WES and NLS surveys.

OCCUPATIONAL DISTRIBUTIONS: A BACKGROUND FOR COMPARISONS

There are some broad similarities between the occupations of women in Britain and the USA. Previous attempts at comparisons have floundered on the different occupational categories used in the two countries. We are able to overcome this limitation with our data from the WES and NLS surveys. Since both surveys can be seen to reflect women's national occupational distributions in the two countries these results are of general national significance. The results in Chapter 2 illustrate that women in both countries had a high proportion in clerical work, and younger women to a greater extent than older women, again in both countries. Clerical work occupied a larger proportion of American than British women although the gap between them was much reduced in the younger age group. The other major difference between American and British women was in the proportion of women in semi-skilled factory and unskilled work. These were much greater in Britain than in the USA but, as with clerical work, the gap had declined in the younger age group as British women's proportion in semi-skilled factory and unskilled work had declined. When we compared the age group changes within a country British women appeared to have been experiencing more occupational changes across the age groups than did women in the USA. We were not able to say from these aggregate figures whether these changes were life cycle (or age) effects, or whether the changes are generational. If they are life cycle (or age) effects we would expect younger British women to become more like older British women over time. If they are generational effects we would expect them to reflect secular changes in women's experiences which are linked to changes in employment opportunities. The rest of our analysis will begin to separate these effects by comparing different age groups over the same life-cycle transition.

Hakim (1979) has made some comparisons of the way British and American women are distributed through the occupational structure in the two countries. She compared the figures quoted in some American sources with her own analysis of British (and US) Census data. The sources she used for US women were Oppenheimer (1970), Ehrlich *et al.* (1975), Williams (1976) and Gross (1968). Hakim's main conclusions are listed below. It is important to recognise that her comparisons only go up to 1970. Hakim concluded that:

1. Britain and the USA are alike in that women are concentrated into occupations which are disproportionately 'female'.
2. Over the period 1900–70, a greater amount of change can be seen in the USA than in Britain. Women had higher participation rates in the USA than in Britain by 1970 and the over-representation of women in disproportionately 'female' jobs declined in the USA between 1900 and 1970 to a greater extent than occurred in Britain. The USA started off having more occupational segregation than Britain but overtook Britain in progress towards occupational desegregation by 1961.
3. Occupational segregation has not changed very much in Britain over this century.
4. The changing pattern of the occupational distribution has been similar in Britain and the USA between 1940 and 1970. Women

have been increasingly employed in clerical, sales and service work occupations, and women constitute the whole of the private household workers in both countries.

5. The proportion of women in professional work (lower and higher grades) declined in both countries between 1940 and 1970.

6. The changes in occupational segregation which occurred up to 1970 were similar in the USA and Britain; men made inroads into women's preserves but the reverse did not happen to the same extent.

7. More recent studies in both Britain (Hakim, 1981) and the USA (Beller, 1982, 1982a; England, 1982) of occupational segregation have found that changes have occurred during the 1970s; the same in both countries. These studies found that occupational segregation declined in the 1970s – sometimes since 1967 – but only until 1977. Since 1977 occupational segregation has been increasing largely because of the recession of the late 1970s. Studies of the USA identified the source of change up to 1977 as the increased probability that women would be working in a male occupation, sometimes called 'atypical' women's occupations as opposed to 'typical' ones.[1] Both the British and American studies suggest that part of the cause of the change was the legislation on civil rights and equal opportunities in Britain and the USA.

Against this background we can begin to examine the occupational mobility of the British and American women in our two surveys. Hakim's conclusion (1979) points us in the direction we wish to take as she says:

occupational segregation cannot be understood in terms of women giving priority to their family responsibilities, their lower take-up of educational and training facilities, or prejudice against working women. All of these are explanations which focus on individual motivation, ambition, and attitudes. While these must play a part, cross-national comparisons suggest that both structural and historical factors must also contribute to an explanation of trends in the degree and pattern of occupational segregation (Hakim, 1975, p. 43).

We will briefly summarise some of the major findings and conclusions of other British and American studies of occupational mobility before we discuss our own findings.

OCCUPATIONAL MOBILITY STUDIES

There are a growing number of studies of women's occupational mobility although not many focus particularly on the family formation period. It is more common to find studies of large-scale data where aggregate methods are used and conclusions are inferred about women's occupational mobility over family formation. The nature of the data is the main reason for the methods of analysis used.

Studies of occupational mobility in the USA have compared women's and men's occupational attainment. They have often been concerned to explain the failure of women's occupational profiles to reach the same levels of attainment as those of men. Some recent studies have conducted an investigation of occupational attainment in the context of a series of job transitions over time (Tuma, 1976; Felmlee, 1982) or as an explication of the concept of a career (Sorensen, 1977; Spilerman, 1977; Rosenfeld, 1979, 1980). These studies have found that women fail to make gains in status because of discontinuities in their employment to some extent. The discontinuities are then assumed to be caused by family formation. The studies also show, however, that the differences between men's and women's work histories are only part of the explanation of the status or wage gap between them,[2] and that women receive lower returns to their human capital. Women have been found to have fewer opportunities for gains in occupational status over their life course, and women's occupational attainment seems to depend more on formal qualifications than on previous achievements in the labour force. A study of job-changing within and between firms by Felmlee (1982) found that job-changing within a firm was better for women's prospects and occupational attainment than job-changing between firms. Here again women can be assumed to be at a disadvantage if they have discontinuities in their working experiences which mean that they have more between-firm job-changing. Shaw (1983) demonstrated that American women's occupational segregation over childbirth did not change very significantly, but that women who did have children had less chance of entering the non-traditional jobs opening up which continuous workers were able to enter. One study in the USA has specifically attempted to examine the effects of motherhood using the number of childbirths (Sorensen, 1983) and has found that children may primarily affect the timing of their mother's career but not her gains in status once she has decided to return to the labour force.

Studies in Britain touching on occupational mobility have documented the downgrading which women experience at some points in their life cycle. Joshi's (1984) analysis of the WES data found that 18 per cent of women whose highest occupational classification by 1980 was in teaching were currently (or recently) in a lower-ranking occupation and the equivalent percentage for women whose highest occupation was nursing or intermediate non-manual work was 39 per cent. Elias (1983) has documented more of this occupational downgrading from the National Training Survey data, as have Stewart and Greenhalgh (1982, 1984).

Occupational downgrading in Britain has also been linked to discontinuities in women's labour-force experience. Stewart and Greenhalgh (1982) found that 25 per cent of women aged 45–54 with an uninterrupted work history were in managerial, professional or technical occupations whereas only 13 per cent of women of this age group were in this occupation when they had two or more breaks from work. Their general conclusions were that job continuity tends to preserve occupational position and breaks in employment are associated with downward occupational mobility. Elias (1983) extended this work on the same data and reached similar conclusions. In all cases, women's breaks from employment are assumed to be because of childbirth.

Some recent British analyses of the WES data have specifically examined occupational change between the last job before childbirth and the first job after (Dex, 1984; Martin and Roberts, 1984). These studies have documented that downward occupational mobility takes place at this time, but also some upward occupational mobility takes place. Dex (1983) has also shown that women experience a large amount of occupational mobility at other times in their life as well as over family formation. The length of time not working over the first break for childbirth was found to have some relationship to the occurrence of downward occupational mobility; longer durations of not working seem to be associated with downward occupational mobility although this relationship was not tested in a multivariate model. Martin and Roberts' analysis (1984) shows that there is an association between downward occupational mobility and the part-time jobs which women take on their first return to work. Shaw's analysis (1983a) of the young NLS women in the USA found that the individual woman seeking a part-time job was more likely to find one in a 'typical' rather than an 'atypical' occupation although the opportunity for part-time work did exist in many 'atypical' occupations.

These British and American studies point to a set of relationships which British and American women have in common, whereby occupational downward mobility does occur because of the breaks from work at childbirth, and the experience of downward occupational mobility has some relationship to the length of time not working at this point, and – in Britain – to whether a woman has a part-time job on her return to work. Further work needs to establish the extent of this occupational mobility and weight the different factors which are thought to have some influence in this experience. In addition a comparison between British and American experiences of occupational mobility over family formation will enable us to see the role played by the structure of employment *vis à vis* the other supply factors. Our analysis contributes to furthering the understanding of women's occupational mobility in these directions.

THE WES AND NLS SURVEYS

The main details about comparing the information from the two surveys are outlined below:

1. The WES occupational categories were twelve in number. The NLS data contained a much finer occupational classification from the US Census. It was possible therefore to reclassify the US occupations using the twelve WES codes.
2. The usual definitions of part-time work differ in the two countries. In Britain part-time work is generally defined as 30 hours or less whereas in the USA, the standard definition is less than 35 hours. The US data contained the detailed number of hours worked so that the British definition could be used to define the part-time category. Where the WES work-history data are used, women were asked to define themselves as working either part- or full-time so that the British data are not so precisely defined in terms of hours worked. Some analysis was done on the hours-worked distributions in 1980 or 1979 to see how they compared. The differences found between British and American women in this respect were far too great to be caused by minor differences of definition, however. We have adopted the British definition of

part-time work in our comparisons recognising however that the distributions of actual hours worked where women were working at the 1980 interview vary between Britain and the USA as Table 2.2 illustrates.

3. The occupation of the first return to work after childbirth was not known precisely for all women in the American sample so that this table is provided for the British older women only.

4. The tables are based on restricted samples, as appropriate, in that it is obvious that it is only those who have not only had a child but have also returned to work at least once after childbirth whose occupational mobility across childbirth can be examined. In the case of the younger women, some of them were still in the process of family formation when they were interviewed in 1980. As the figures in Tables 2.3 and 2.7 illustrate, 16 per cent of the younger British women's cohort had never had a child by 1980 and a further 23 per cent had had a child but never returned. A total of 39 per cent were excluded from this analysis of mobility; the equivalent proportion of American women is 38.2 per cent. A comparison of the first jobs of women included in and excluded from the sample was made for the British cohort of younger women and the figures are displayed in Appendix Table B6. There are some important differences between these two distributions. The excluded group were in the higher-grade occupations (non-manual) to a far larger extent than those who have already returned after childbirth. This result coincides with what we would expect; women who delay their childbirth are likely to do so largely because the opportunity cost of not working is higher for them, their incomes being greater. Biases may be introduced into the analysis from women not having the completed experiences of family formation but this is a common and unavoidable problem in analysing longitudinal data. The similar proportions of British and American women who are affected suggest that any biasing effects will be similar.

LAST JOB BEFORE AND FIRST JOB AFTER CHILDBIRTH

We have the details of the younger women's occupations either side of childbirth; in their last job before childbirth and their first job after childbirth. A summary of the distributions through the twelve British occupational categories at each of these points is provided in Table

TABLE 4.1   *Younger women: occupational distributions of women at key points*
(Percentages in each occupation)

Occupation	Last job before first child		First job after first child		Those who worked after first child Most recent job 1980	
	British	American	British	American	British	American
Professional	0.6	0.8	0.5	1.4	0.5	1.1
Teacher	4.7	8.6	4.3	8.0	4.7	8.4
Nurse	6.8	8.0	6.9	8.1	7.4	8.2
Intermediate non-manual	2.7	3.7	2.6	4.3	3.8	7.2
Clerical	34.1	38.0	19.2	33.2	22.2	33.8
Sales	13.9	6.1	12.8	7.9	9.7	6.8
Skilled	9.0	5.5	7.1	7.2	6.5	8.7
Child care	0.5	4.1	3.1	3.1	3.7	1.8
Semi-skilled factory	20.5	10.1	17.8	10.2	12.8	9.3
Semi-skilled domestic	2.7	8.3	12.8	8.5	12.7	7.0
Other semi-skilled	3.8	4.9	4.3	6.6	4.7	6.2
Unskilled	0.7	1.9	8.7	1.5	11.4	1.5
Total	100.0	100.0	100.0	100.0	100.0	100.0
N =	844	1553	859	1553	860	1548
Not available	16		1			

SAMPLE   Women with at least one child who have returned to work after childlbirth.

4.1 for younger women in each sample who had returned to work after childbirth at least once. In part the distributions reflect some of the features of the British and American occupational structure for women which we noted in Chapter 2; namely, that American women are more predominantly in clerical work and less in semi-skilled factory, sales and sometimes unskilled work than are British women. These distributions also show that American women have higher proportions as a whole than British women in higher grade semi-professional occupations – that is, as teachers, nurses and intermediate non-manual workers.

Some notable changes occur when we compare these aggregate

level distributions before and after childbirth. Both countries experience a decline in the proportion in clerical work although the fall is far more dramatic in the British data. The proportion in semi-skilled factory work in Britain also falls after childbirth although in the USA there is no change. The US changes can be summarised as being a fall in clerical work which is balanced by an increase in semi-skilled jobs (sales included) with no change in higher-grade occupations. In the British data the large fall in clerical and semi-skilled factory work is taken up by large increases in semi-skilled domestic and unskilled work. It is worth noting that these results cast a new light on the previous comparisons of British and American women's most recent jobs where British women had much higher proportions in unskilled work. These figures demonstrate that the phenomenon is associated with the post-childbirth phase of women's work since British women, like American women, rarely work in unskilled occupations prior to childbirth.

The examination of these summary tables suggests that British women experience a lot of occupational change over their family formation phase, whereas for American women the changes are not so great. We would be wrong to draw this conclusion from aggregate level distributions however, and a more detailed examination of the occupational changes which lie behind these summary distributions proves this point only too well.

The detailed matrix of occupational changes between the last birth before and first return after childbirth for younger women are outlined in Tables 4.2 and 4.3 for British and American women respectively. There is a large amount of detail contained in these tables which we will only summarise here. It is clear from a comparison of the diagonal elements which show how many women stay in the same occupation before and after childbirth that the impression gained from the aggregate distributions was incorrect; it is not clearly the case that British women experience more mobility than US women over their family-formation period. In teaching and intermediate non-manual jobs British women have far less movement than American women. (We are unable to compare the professional category because there are so few British women in this occupation.) From nursing and clerical work there is more movement by British women and in the rest of the semi-skilled jobs and skilled occupations the mobility is about the same, but British unskilled workers are far more likely than American unskilled workers to remain unskilled.

TABLE 4.2 Occupation of last job before childbirth and first job after, for younger British women
(Shown as percentages)

Last job before childbirth \ First return job	Professional	Teacher	Nurse	Intermediate non-manual	Clerical	Sales	Skilled	Child care	Semi-skilled factory	Semi-skilled domestic	Other semi-skilled	Unskilled	Total %	N
Professional	80	–	–	–	20	–	–	–	–	–	–	–	100	5*
Teacher	–	83	5	5	–	3	3	3	–	–	–	–	100	40
Nurse	–	2	72	–	4	4	4	2	–	11	2	2	100	57
Intermediate non-manual	–	4	4	48	17	13	–	4	–	4	–	4	100	23
Clerical	–	1	2	2	49	13	3	4	7	12	2	7	100	288
Sales	–	–	3	–	7	33	3	3	17	16	8	11	100	117
Skilled	–	–	1	3	5	9	50	4	11	8	3	7	100	76
Child care	–	–	–	–	–	50	–	25	25	–	–	–	100	4*
Semi-skilled factory	–	–	2	–	1	10	2	2	51	15	5	11	100	173
Semi-skilled domestic	–	–	4	4	4	9	13	–	4	52	–	9	100	23
Other semi-skilled	–	–	3	–	3	–	3	6	19	13	31	22	100	32
Unskilled	–	–	–	–	–	–	–	–	17	17	–	67	100	6*
Percentage of first return jobs which are part-time	(100)	59	73	64	61	67	60	89	58	92	70	97		844

SAMPLE Women with at least one childbirth who have ever returned to work since childbirth.

* Note the extremely small cell sizes of figures in this row.

TABLE 4.3 Occupation of last job before childbirth and first job after for younger American women

First return job / Last job before childbirth	Professional	Teacher	Nurse	Intermediate non-manual	Clerical	Sales	Skilled	Child-care	Semi-skilled factory	Semi-skilled domestic	Other semi-skilled	Unskilled	Total %	N
Professional	73	–	9	9	–	–	–	–	9	–	–	–	100	12*
Teacher	2	69	–	5	10	3	1	3	1	3	4	–	100	123
Nurse	–	–	90	2	4	3	–	–	–	–	–	1	100	98
Intermediate non-manual	10	6	2	31	21	12	7	3	2	4	2	–	100	55
Clerical	–	3	–	4	65	8	3	2	4	5	5	1	100	571
Sales	–	3	2	9	26	28	9	2	6	4	10	–	100	86
Skilled	–	4	2	–	13	6	55	2	4	11	2	2	100	79
Child care	–	–	2	2	20	8	6	26	13	16	2	4	100	65
Semi-skilled factory	1	2	–	2	11	5	4	6	55	5	6	3	100	169
Semi-skilled domestic	–	2	3	3	15	6	11	–	13	40	5	2	100	148
Other semi-skilled	–	2	1	–	16	4	3	2	13	12	44	4	100	112
Unskilled	–	–	1	5	18	10	18	–	8	20	3	16	100	35
Percentage of first return jobs which are part-time	24	44	42	43	33	69	47	40	11	54	46	48		

SAMPLE Women with at least one childbirth who have ever returned to work since childbirth.
* Note the small cell sizes of figures in this row.

The fact that the USA total distributions before and after child-birth change to a lesser extent than the British ones suggests that the movements which take place in the USA balance each other out to a greater extent than they do in Britain so that the net effect appears to be less overall mobility in the USA. For every movement out of the semi-skilled occupation there is a movement in. This process can also be seen to be occurring with clerical work in the USA. The column figures show the relative size of inflow into this occupation and there is considerable inflow into clerical work at the first return to work from all occupations in the USA. (By comparison, in Britain the inflow is tiny.) Much of this inflow into clerical work in both countries comes from occupations which are likely to be ranked below clerical work so that at least some of this mobility is upwards occupational mobility. We can deduce from these results that there is a greater supply of clerical jobs for women with children in the USA than there is in Britain.

Not surprisingly, the most stable occupations in both countries are the higher-grade semi-professional and professional occupations. The most mobile occupations are the same in both Britain and the USA; they are sales, child care and, to a lesser extent, semi-skilled domestic occupations in the USA and other semi-skilled occupations in Britain. Unskilled work is also highly mobile in the USA but is such a small category in Britain that we are unable to make comparisons. These results are not unexpected and they fit in with what we know about the nature of women's career opportunities in both countries.

The two other major occupations into which women flow after childbirth are also shared by both countries; these are semi-skilled factory and semi-skilled domestic work. Since these occupations are towards the bottom of the ranking structure, some of the inflow occurs from downward occupational mobility from other occupations.

In an overall sense there are different occupational routes which women take over this period between the two countries. If we examine the modal percentage in each row, excluding the diagonal element, we can see where most women move to and these occupations are quite different for Britain and the USA. In Britain the most common routes are downward movements in the occupational hierarchy, whereas in the USA, there is a large flow into clerical work which in many cases might be upward mobility. In Britain, although the figures are based on small cell sizes, women stay in unskilled work and the inflow to that occupation is also greater suggesting that unskilled work in Britain seems to be particularly reserved for women returning to work after childbirth.

VERTICAL OCCUPATIONAL MOBILITY

If we are to examine occupational mobility more precisely we need to define which occupational movements constitute either upwards or downwards occupational mobility. The ranking we have adopted for this set of twelve WES occupational categories is one which approximately overlaps with the ranking of these occupations by their earnings, in Joshi (1984), and which corresponds with the occupational profiles described in another analysis of the WES in Dex (1984a). The ranking, starting at the highest, is as follows:

1. Professional or teaching
2. Nursing
3. Intermediate non-manual work
4. Clerical
5. Skilled
6. Semi-skilled factory
7. All other occupations (that is, sales, child care, semi-skilled domestic, other semi-skilled, unskilled)

Downward (or upward) vertical occupational mobility for the purposes of this analysis is defined as movement either down (or up) on the above scale.

A summary of the upward and downward occupational mobility between the last job before and first job after childbirth is provided in Figure 4.1 and Appendix Table B7. These results illustrate more clearly that British women experience less downward mobility than American women in teaching. Since some of the cell sizes are small it seemed best to aggregate the higher-grade occupations above clerical work, and when this is done the amount of downward mobility in the two countries is fairly similar. But from clerical work downwards, American women clearly experience less downward mobility and far more upward mobility. In fact American women experience considerable amounts of upward mobility over this period and far more than British women irrespective of their original occupation. The conclusion of this comparison is that American women do not maintain their occupational position over the family-formation phase by

88

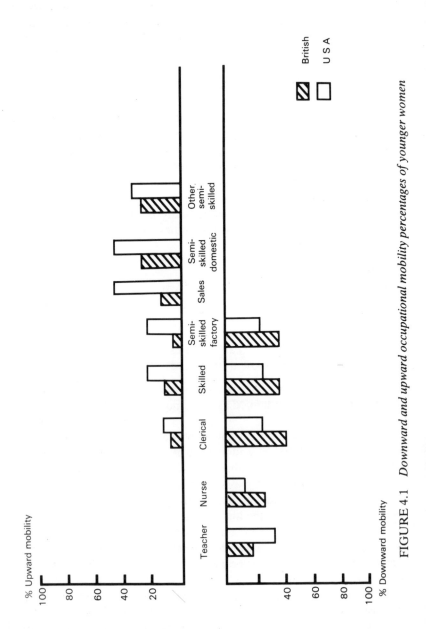

FIGURE 4.1 *Downward and upward occupational mobility percentages of younger women*

experiencing less mobility, but by women in lower-level jobs experiencing less downward mobility than British women and more upward mobility. Of course, these lower-level jobs are the ones which most women have. One of the major factors differentiating British and American women which underlies these results is that in the USA far more clerical jobs appear to be available for women returning to work after childbirth than in Britain.

We can add a further dimension to this comparison by examining the status of the jobs to which women return after childbirth. The proportions of each returning occupation which were part-time are displayed along the bottom rows of Tables 4.2 and 4.3. There are higher proportions of part-time jobs in almost every occupation in Britain than is the case in the USA and in many cases the differences are considerable, almost double. Even the ranking differs between the two countries so that, for example, in Britain the largest proportions of part-time work appear to be in semi-skilled domestic (92 per cent), unskilled (97 per cent) and child-care occupations (89 per cent), followed by nursing and other semi-skilled work (70–3 per cent). In the USA the largest proportions are in sales (69 per cent), followed by semi-skilled domestic (54 per cent) and unskilled (48 per cent). There is some relationship therefore with the destination occupations of the downwardly mobile and part-time working status in Britain, and on the other hand, full-time working status and upward mobility into clerical work in the USA where only 33 per cent of returning clerical jobs are part-time. We cannot be more precise about this relationship here although we will take up the issue of part-time work again later in this chapter. We can note the importance of different structures of job opportunities and part-time work for women returners in the USA and in Britain which lie behind these results.

YOUNGER WOMEN'S MOST RECENT JOBS

With our longitudinal data we can follow these young women further on in their working experiences after their first return to work. We have examined the occupations of their most recent jobs in 1980 and have compared them with their occupations before the start of family formation (for women who had had a child and who had never returned to work since). The distributions of most recent jobs in total were displayed in Table 4.1. In addition matrices of occupational changes between the last job before the first birth and the most recent jobs are provided for the British and American samples of younger women in Tables 4.4 and 4.5.

From the total distributions in Table 4.1 we can see that there is some overall improvement in the position of both British and American women when comparing the first job after childbirth with the most recent job. In both countries women have slightly higher proportions in non-manual jobs and slightly lower proportions in semi-skilled manual jobs; there is an exception in the British case in that 'most recent' jobs have a higher proportion of unskilled work than 'first return' jobs. Semi-skilled factory work has an even smaller percentage in the most recent job distribution than it had in the 'first return' jobs so that there is a progressive decline over the life cycle of employment in semi-skilled factory work. These results suggest that British women have experienced some upward occupational mobility between their first return and most recent job. By comparison with their last job before childbirth, British women are still in a worse position in their most recent jobs, having lost a sizeable proportion in clerical, skilled and semi-skilled factory work and gained jobs in semi-skilled domestic and unskilled work with only very small increases in higher-grade occupations. In the USA however the smaller loss of clerical jobs is approximately counterbalanced by an increase in intermediate non-manual jobs and other semi-professional jobs.

The figures in Tables 4.4 and 4.5 show more of the details of these changes for the younger cohorts. A comparison between British and American changes now shows that the American women tend to be clearly more mobile out of teaching, intermediate non-manual and semi-skilled domestic work than British women (as seen in the relative size of the diagonal elements), but British women are more mobile out of semi-skilled factory and skilled occupations than American women, presumably because of the greater decline in manufacturing in Britain. The dominant shifts are the same as between the last job and first return job after childbirth but if anything more marked; a massive inflow into clerical work occurred in the USA and lesser inflows into semi-skilled factory, skilled and semi-skilled domestic, and in Britain predominant inflows into semi-skilled domestic and unskilled work; some of these shifts are offset by movements in or out of the occupation in the opposite direction. The net effect on clerical work in the USA because of the out- and inflows is an overall decrease as we saw from the figures in Table 4.1. The proportion of part-time work has gone down in the 'most recent' jobs

TABLE 4.4 Occupational mobility from last job before childbirth to most recent job (1980) of younger British women (as percentages)

Last job before childbirth \ Most recent job	Professional	Teacher	Nurse	Intermediate non-manual	Clerical	Sales	Skilled	Child care	Semi-skilled factory	Semi-skilled domestic	Other semi-skilled	Unskilled	Total %	N =
Professional	80	–	–	–	20	–	–	–	–	–	–	–	100	5
Teacher	–	83	3	3	–	–	3	3	–	–	3	–	100	40
Nurse	–	2	75	–	2	4	2	–	2	11	2	2	100	57
Intermediate non-manual	–	4	–	48	26	4	–	–	9	9	–	–	100	23
Clerical	–	1	2	4	53	9	4	5	6	9	2	6	100	289
Sales	–	–	3	3	8	22	7	4	13	15	7	18	100	117
Skilled	–	1	–	5	8	11	36	5	8	12	1	13	100	76
Child care	–	–	–	–	–	50	–	25	–	25	–	–	100	4
Semi-skilled factory	–	–	4	1	8	9	4	4	32	15	8	17	100	173
Semi-skilled domestic	–	–	–	4	4	9	9	–	–	48	4	22	100	23
Other semi-skilled	–	3	3	–	6	3	3	3	16	16	19	31	100	32
Unskilled	–	–	33	–	–	–	–	–	33	33	–	–	100	6
Percentage of destination occupations which are part-time	100	53	69	56	61	73	75	88	56	91	62	96		845

SAMPLE Women with at least one childbirth who have ever returned to work.

TABLE 4.5 Occupational mobility from last job before childbirth to most recent job (1980) of younger American women (as percentages)

Last job before childbirth	Professional	Teacher	Nurse	Intermediate non-manual	Clerical	Sales	Skilled	Child care	Semi-skilled factory	Semi-skilled domestic	Other semi-skilled	Unskilled	Total %	N
Professional	43	10	9	9	12	9	–	–	9	–	–	–	100	12
Teacher	–	63	1	9	8	5	4	2	–	2	6	–	100	122
Nurse	2	–	75	6	5	2	1	–	1	4	3	–	100	98
Intermediate non-manual	6	7	2	27	29	5	9	3	2	3	6	1	100	55
Clerical	1	3	2	6	60	7	5	2	4	4	5	1	100	570
Sales	–	7	3	16	29	16	10	–	6	3	8	2	100	85
Skilled	–	4	2	4	12	6	44	2	7	16	2	2	100	79
Child care	–	–	1	4	22	11	12	14	19	13	3	2	100	65
Semi-skilled factory	–	3	–	4	21	7	10	1	40	5	6	2	100	168
Semi-skilled domestic	–	2	9	4	19	7	11	–	15	25	7	1	100	148
Other semi-skilled	–	2	2	4	31	2	4	3	13	13	22	4	100	111
Unskilled	–	–	–	4	19	6	16	5	17	13	8	12	100	35
Percentage working part-time at most recent job	34	40	45	26	31	63	39	44	11	51	56	55	37	1548

SAMPLE Women with at least one childbirth who have ever returned to work.

in most of the British occupational categories, with the prominent exceptions of unskilled and semi-skilled domestic work in Britain which remains almost wholly part-time for these women with children. These results suggest that as British women get older some move out of part-time jobs although if they stay in certain occupations there are only part-time jobs to do. Dex (1984) has shown that there is considerable movement between part- and full-time jobs in women's post-childbirth working experiences in Britain.

Recovery Rates

A summary of the subsequent experiences of the younger women who were downwardly mobile at their first return to work is displayed in Table 4.6. (The figures in column (1) are redisplayed from the

TABLE 4.6 *Experiences of younger women of downward occupational mobility over first break from work for childbirth and later recovery of status*
(as percentages)

Occupation of last job before first birth	*(1)* Proportion of occupation prior to childbirth experiencing downward occupational mobility		*(2)* Proportion of those experiencing downward occupational mobility in Col. (1) who have recovered their status at their most recent job*		*(3)* Proportion of occupation prior to childbirth experiencing downward mobility to a part-time job who recovered their status at the most recent job*	
	British	American	British	American	British	American
Professional	20	(27)	–	–	–	–
Teacher	17	30	43	24	43	32
Nurse	26	10	33	9	27	16
Intermediate non-manual	44	51	–	14	–	19
Clerical	47	28	25	36	21	32
Skilled	41	27	16	32	16	18
Semi-skilled factory	43	25	20	67	20	67

* Most recent job is the one given at the interview in mid-1980 as the most recent.

earlier Figure 4.1.) The most notable difference between British and American women is that British women in clerical, skilled or semi-skilled factory work before childbirth have less chance of recovering their status than American women, if they lost it at their first return to work. Not only do British women experience more downward mobility on their first return to work, they have lower prospects of retrieving their earlier status than the US women.

The last column of Table 4.6 provides the recovery rates for women who were downwardly mobile across childbirth into a part-time job. There are hardly any differences between the figures in columns (2) and (3) which suggests that recovery of one's occupational status after losing it is equally likely irrespective of whether one went into a part-time or full-time job initially after childbirth. In the USA the conclusion applies also to semi-skilled work. By contrast, in the USA recovery of one's occupational status is greater from a part-time job in teaching, nursing or intermediate non-manual work. This is another way in which the structure of part-time work differs between the British and American economies.

YOUNGER AND OLDER BRITISH WOMEN ACROSS THE FIRST BREAK FOR CHILDBIRTH

In the British data we have information about the last job before childbirth and the first job after for both younger and older women. The older women's matrix of occupational changes at this time is displayed in Table 4.7, the equivalent table for the younger women being already displayed in Table 4.2. A comparison of these two cohorts, holding their position in the life-cycle constant, permits us to see more of the generational changes in British women. There is a great measure of similarity between the generations at this time in their life cycle.

The diagonal elements do suggest that some changes have been occurring, however. Nursing, intermediate non-manual, skilled, semi-skilled domestic and other semi-skilled are all more stable occupations in the younger generation than in the older. The other occupations have approximately the same level of attachment across this childbirth break. The net effect of these changes, therefore, is that there has been an increase in occupational attachment across childbirth and slightly less downward occupational mobility. The major destination categories are still similar however in that the

TABLE 4.7 Occupational change between last job before childbirth and first return job of older British women (as percentages)

Last job before childbirth	Professional	Teacher	Nurse	Intermediate non-manual	Clerical	Sales	Skilled	Child care	Semi-skilled factory	Semi-skilled domestic	Other semi-skilled	Unskilled	Total	N=
Professional	100	–	–	–	–	–	–	–	–	–	–	–	100	1
Teacher	–	87	–	–	–	5	5	–	–	–	3	–	100	39
Nurse	–	6	53	–	6	6	8	4	–	12	4	2	100	51
Intermediate non-manual	–	6	–	31	38	19	–	–	–	–	6	–	100	16
Clerical	–	2	3	1	49	15	3	3	6	9	4	5	100	377
Sales	–	1	5	3	10	42	3	3	7	14	3	9	100	147
Skilled	–	–	7	2	7	12	36	3	13	7	2	12	100	106
Child care	–	–	–	–	–	13	13	13	13	25	13	13	100	8
Semi-skilled factory	–	–	1	1	3	11	3	1	50	11	5	14	100	357
Semi-skilled domestic	–	–	2	–	2	6	4	–	22	43	3	19	100	68
Other semi-skilled	–	–	–	1	1	9	4	3	11	13	43	15	100	79
Unskilled	–	–	–	4	4	–	–	–	11	33	11	37	100	27
Percentage of destination occupation in part time work (rounded)	50	50	63	43	61	74	60	83	50	75	61	94	N = 1283 Not available 7	

largest inflow occupations are sales, semi-skilled domestic and un-skilled work in both generations.

The other noteworthy difference between the generations can be seen in the proportions of women in part-time work after childbirth. These proportions are markedly increased on the whole in the younger cohort. The increase in part-time work is by far the greatest in semi-skilled domestic and nursing and it is also large in teaching and intermediate non-manual work. Interestingly, part-time work at this first return to work has hardly increased in clerical work, and has even decreased in sales. Some of these results overlap with what we know has been happening to part-time work in Britain. These results show that women's first return has been increasingly into part-time work and that the increase has come in most occupations, but in some more than others. The fact that semi-skilled domestic work is one of the crucial inflow categories – often after an experience of downward occupational mobility – suggests that another link between part-time work and downward occupational mobility can be seen here.

LAST JOB BEFORE CHILDBIRTH TO MOST RECENT JOB FOR OLDER WOMEN

We can compare the older cohorts of British and American women before and after childbirth but their post-childbirth job is the most recent one rather than their first return job; in some cases the two will be the same. A summary of women's distributions through the occupational categories at these two positions is displayed in Table 4.8. The major categories occurring before and after childbirth in the two countries are identical to those found in the younger age group. In Britain the most recent jobs show a decline in the proportion of clerical and increases in semi-skilled domestic and unskilled work plus an increase in each of the higher-grade occupations, intermediate non-manual or above, which amounts to approximately 6 per cent altogether. In the USA the fall in clerical work is more than balanced by an increase in higher-level jobs. The fact that we have found similar changes to be occurring to different generations of women in each country at approximately the same point in their life cycle suggests that the occupational structures in the British and American economies have become accommodated to women's life-cycle work-ing patterns; in particular to women's discontinuous work over their

TABLE 4.8   *Comparison of last occupation before first birth and most*
recent occupation, for older women
(as percentages)

	Before first birth		Most recent job	
	British	*American*	*British*	*American*
Professional	0.1	0.5	0.2	0.6
Teacher	3.0	5.1	4.2	5.8
Nurse	4.0	4.5	6.0	5.2
Intermediate non-manual	1.2	2.5	4.0	9.8
Clerical	29.4	40.8	21.3	32.6
Sales	11.5	7.2	12.0	8.4
Skilled	8.3	4.6	5.8	8.2
Child care	0.6	0.6	2.5	1.3
Semi-skilled factory	27.8	14.8	15.0	10.9
Semi-skilled domestic	5.3	8.9	12.6	8.1
Other semi-skilled	6.2	9.4	3.7	6.8
Unskilled	2.6	1.1	12.7	2.3
Total	100.0	100.0	100.0	100.0
N =	1283	2171	1311	2171
Not available	28	–	–	–

SAMPLE   Women with at least one child who have ever worked after childbirth.

family-formation phase. However, the structures in Britain and the USA are different from each other.

If we compare these older women with the younger women at the same point in their life cycle – before their first childbirth – from Table 4.1, we can see that some generational and therefore structural changes in the British and American economies have taken place. Most notably in Britain clerical and semi-professional occupations have expanded over time whilst semi-skilled factory work has been declining. In the USA the expanding occupations are similar to the British ones although child care has also been expanding in the USA, but the declining industries for women prior to childbirth in the USA include the other semi-skilled categories as well as semi-skilled factory work (but not sales).

The detailed matrices of occupational transitions for older women are displayed in Tables 4.9 and 4.10. American women are more mobile out of professional, teaching and sales, less mobile out of skilled work and fairly similar to British older women in other respects between these pre- and post-childbirth occupations. Mobility in both countries was greater on the whole out of lower-level occupations than higher ones. The occupations into which British women flow after childbirth were unskilled, semi-skilled domestic, semi-skilled factory occupations and to a lesser extent sales. Semi-skilled factory work was not such an important inflow category in the younger British cohort which confirms that it has declined. In the USA as previously, the predominant inflow category was clerical work but considerable movement into semi-skilled factory and semi-skilled domestic work also occurred. In all but one occupation the proportions of part-time work were greater in Britain than in the USA as with the younger cohorts. In summary, there is slightly more occupational mobility in the USA than in Britain over this period from before childbirth to a considerable time afterwards. The mobility over this longer period is less than that seen over the shorter period either side of the break for childbirth. The results confirm therefore that there is some measure of recovery of status in the post-childbirth working experience.

The total percentages of upward and downward mobility over this period are displayed in Figure 4.2 and Appendix Table B8. As with the younger cohorts we can see in the figures that American women have more downward mobility from the top occupations but less downward mobility from the lower-level occupations, from clerical work downwards, in comparison with British women. American women have far more upward mobility than British women in nearly all cases although the differences are particularly marked at the lower occupational levels. American women's greater mobility than that of British women across their family-formation phase appears to be a distinct advantage to them since more of it consists in upward occupational mobility. Two facts help to explain these differences; the fact that far more British women are in part-time jobs than are US women, and, as we saw in Chapter 3, that American women spend less time out of work on average over their family-formation break than British women.

We can now examine more precisely the influence of these differences between British and American women in their experiences of downward occupational mobility.

TABLE 4.9 Occupational change between last job before first birth and most recent job (1980) of older British women (as percentages)

Last job before childbirth	Professional	Teacher	Nurse	Intermediate non-manual	Clerical	Sales	Skilled	Child care	Semi-skilled factory	Semi-skilled domestic	Other semi-skilled	Unskilled	Total %	N
Professional	100	–	–	–	–	–	–	–	–	–	–	–	100	1
Teacher	–	80	5	–	3	8	3	–	–	–	3	–	100	39
Nurse	–	8	55	4	6	4	2	6	2	8	2	4	100	51
Intermediate non-manual	6	13	6	19	31	13	–	–	6	–	6	–	100	16
Clerical	–	3	3	7	51	12	4	2	5	6	2	4	100	377
Sales	–	1	7	7	18	29	5	2	5	12	3	13	100	147
Skilled	–	2	10	5	9	9	19	4	13	9	3	17	100	106
Child care	–	13	13	–	–	38	–	–	25	–	–	13	100	8
Semi-skilled factory	–	–	2	1	8	11	6	2	31	17	4	20	100	357
Semi-skilled domestic	–	–	3	–	9	3	7	6	24	30	–	18	100	68
Other semi-skilled	–	–	3	1	6	9	4	3	22	20	17	17	100	79
Unskilled	–	–	–	4	–	11	7	–	21	14	7	36	100	28
Percentage in part-time in most recent occupation	67	41	57	18	45	75	51	88	36	75	69	86	100	1277

SAMPLE All women with at least one child who have returned to work after childbirth.

TABLE 4.10 Occupational change between last job before first birth and most recent job (1979) of older American women (as percentage)

Last job before childbirth	Professional	Teacher	Nurse	Intermediate non-manual	Clerical	Sales	Skilled	Child care	Semi-skilled factory	Semi-skilled domestic	Other semi-skilled	Unskilled	Total %	N
Professional	12	22	10	12	23	11	–	–	–	–	11	–	100	9
Teacher	2	65	1	10	11	5	1	–	1	4	–	–	100	107
Nurse	–	7	59	5	8	6	3	–	1	5	6	–	100	88
Intermediate non-manual	4	6	7	21	32	11	2	–	7	3	5	1	100	50
Clerical	1	4	2	12	54	9	4	1	4	3	5	1	100	757
Sales	–	2	6	10	21	18	11	3	11	11	5	2	100	137
Skilled	–	–	3	8	22	8	26	–	12	10	3	7	100	95
Child care	–	–	13	9	3	–	7	–	33	24	11	–	100	15
Semi-skilled factory	–	–	1	8	16	8	15	2	34	8	5	4	100	312
Semi-skilled domestic	–	1	5	9	17	4	8	4	15	27	6	4	100	288
Other semi-skilled	–	1	2	3	21	7	13	1	11	14	24	3	100	267
Unskilled	1	–	7	2	32	3	12	–	4	21	11	8	100	46
Percentage working part time at most recent job	35	29	17	27	30	49	37	31	12	53	38	45	32	2171

SAMPLE All women with at least one child who have returned to work after childbirth.

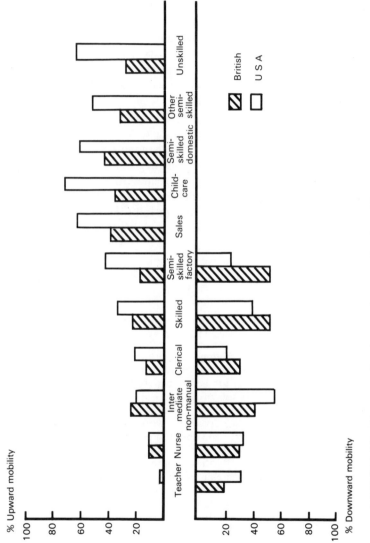

% Upward mobility

100
80
60
40
20

% Downward mobility

20
40
60
80
100

Teacher Nurse

Inter mediate non-manual

Clerical

Skilled

Semi-skilled factory

Sales

Child-care

Semi-skilled domestic

Other semi-skilled

Unskilled

British

USA

FIGURE 4.2 *Downward and upward occupational mobility percentages of older women*

DETERMINANTS OF DOWNWARD OCCUPATIONAL MOBILITY

We have conducted a multivariate analysis of the determinants of women's experiences of downward occupational mobility on the samples of younger women in Britain and the USA. A dependent dichotomous variable was constructed according to whether a woman had experienced downward occupational mobility using the definition already described earlier in this chapter and a regression analysis was carried out. According to our occupational ranking, women could have experienced downward occupational mobility if they were in the occupations of semi-skilled factory work or above before childbirth. We examined whether a woman's experience of downward occupational mobility between her last job before childbirth and her first job after childbirth was related to her occupation before childbirth, her duration of time out of the labour market, and whether she returned to a part-time or full-time job. A full set of the variables included with their precise definitions is provided in Table 4.11.

Given that the variable we are seeking to explain – downward occupational mobility – is dichotomous, taking the value of zero or 1,

TABLE 4.11   *List of variables in regression on downward occupational mobility*

DOWN	Dichotomous dependent variable = 1 if woman experienced downward occupational mobility between last job before childbirth and first job after
PART	If job of first return after childbirth is part-time, variable = 1, zero if full-time
TIME	Time spent not working between date of birth of first child and first return to work, to nearest year
OCC1	Occupational dummy variable = 1 if last job before first birth was either professional or teacher
OCC2	Occupational dummy variable = 1 if last job before first birth was nurse
OCC3	Occupational dummy variable = 1 if last job before first birth was intermediate non-manual
OCC4	Occupational dummy variable = 1 if last job before first birth was clerical
OCC5	Occupational dummy variable = 1 if last job before first birth was skilled

* Excluded occupational dummy = semi-skilled factory

TABLE 4.12 *Regression results on the determinants of downward*
occupational mobility across the first break for childbirth
(t values in parentheses)

Independent variables	British		American	
	OLS	logit*	OLS	logit**
PART	0.254 (6.4)	0.306 (6.1)	0.164 (5.8)	0.158 (5.3)
TIME	0.026 (5.2)	0.028 (4.9)	0.025 (4.0)	0.025 (3.9)
OCC1	−0.196 (2.5)	−0.263 (2.5)	−0.003 (0.1)	0.001 (0.0)
OCC2	−0.110 (1.6)	−0.128 (1.5)	−0.176 (3.3)	−0.223 (2.9)
OCC3	0.037 (0.4)	0.043 (0.4)	0.209 (3.0)	0.219 (3.3)
OCC4	0.028 (0.6)	0.030 (0.6)	−0.018 (0.5)	−0.021 (0.5)
OCC5	0.010 (0.2)	0.013 (0.2)	0.001 (0.0)	0.033 (0.5)
CONSTANT	0.143 (3.2)	–	0.176 (4.8)	–
$\bar{R}^2$	0.130	–	0.082	–
−2 × logLR	–	918.9	–	1082.5
N	679	679	1024	1024

* Adjusted by $p\,(1-p)$. Mean $p = 0.41$
** Adjusted by $p\,(1-p)$. Mean $p = 0.261$

a logit regression analysis should be carried out on the data.[3] We
have calculated both logit coefficients and ordinary least squares
(OLS) regression coefficients to investigate these relationships. Usually one expects that the OLS coefficients will be approximately equal
to the logit results although the size of the OLS coefficients should be
regarded as approximate. Several models were estimated. The results
which are not reported contained more variables; namely, race (for
the USA), family formation patterns, the unemployment rate and
previous work experience. We are reporting the simpler model since
the additional variables did not improve the model with respect to
our main interest, the effect of part-time work. Some of the additional variables like the unemployment rate were difficult to inter-
pret. A list of the regression results for the British and American
samples of younger women are displayed in Table 4.12 and the means
of the variables are provided in Appendix Table B9. The logit
coefficients have been adjusted in the usual way by $p(1-p)$ using the
mean of the dependent variable for p, to make them equivalent and
therefore comparable with the OLS results. The unadjusted logit
coefficients are displayed in Appendix Table B10.

The likelihood of experiencing downward occupational mobility
clearly increased if the first return job is part-time. The amount of the

increase is as much as 31 per cent for British women and 16 per cent for Americans. Taking a part-time job on returning to work after childbirth therefore has serious consequences in both Britain and the USA, although, as we already know, on the whole it is British women who take this option and the effect is considerably greater in Britain.[4] Every additional year spent out of work before the first return also increases the likelihood of experiencing downward occupational mobility on one's return by the same amount for both British and American women – nearly 3 per cent.

British and American women differ slightly in the effects of their previous occupations on occupational mobility at this time. Teachers and nurses appeared to be very unlikely to experience downward occupational mobility in Britain, a result which is confirmed by our earlier examination of the occupational transitions over this break from work. The likelihood of downward occupational mobility from the other occupations turns out to be insignificantly different from semi-skilled factory work in Britain. American women are least likely to experience downward mobility at this time if they were in nursing before childbirth, and they were most likely to have this experience from a position in intermediate non-manual work. Clerical and skilled workers in the USA have insignificantly different experiences from semi-skilled factory workers; in this respect Britain and the USA are similar.

This set of variables only explains a fairly small amount of the variation in women's experiences of occupational mobility across childbirth, but they are all very significant. We might have expected that the higher one's original occupation, the more likely one would be to experience downward occupational mobility, but these results show that there is no necessary relationship of this kind. In Britain it is almost the reverse, and the higher one's occupation the greater one's security of keeping it. This analysis, of course, is not able to examine any changes in occupational status which may have taken place within an occupational category, so we only have a part of the story here, and there may be considerably more experiences of downward occupational mobility than we are capturing. Part-time teachers in Britain, for example, are usually paid at the lowest point on the scale.

Using the equations predicting downward occupational mobility, we can determine how much of the difference between the two countries is the result of differences in the means of the explanatory variables in these equations.[5] Table 4.13 shows the results of this

TABLE 4.13 *Estimated effects on downward occupational mobility of differences between British and American women's characteristics*

	Using British equation[a]		Using American equation[b]	
	Absolute difference	*Percentage of observed difference*	*Absolute difference*	*Percentage of observed difference*
PART	0.077	52	0.050	33
TIME	0.058	40	0.055	37
Occupational differences[c]	0.009	6	0.003	2
Total	0.144	97	0.108	72
Observed difference	0.149	100	0.149	100

[a] Calculated as: $b_B(\bar{X}_B - \bar{X}_U)$ where b_B = coefficients in British equation from Table 4.12, $\bar{X}_B$ = means of British variables, and $\bar{X}_U$ = means of American variables in Appendix Table B9.
[b] Calculated as: $b_U(\bar{X}_B - \bar{X}_U)$.
[c] Sum of differences attributable to *OCC1–OCC5*.

calculation. The first two columns show the added amount (in absolute values and in percentages) of downward mobility that British women have because of their greater propensity to work part-time, their longer absence from the labour force, and the kinds of occupations they hold. The third and fourth columns show the added amount of downward mobility that American women would have if their hours of work, absence from the labour force, and occupations were the same as those of British women.

Using the British coefficients, we see that almost the entire difference in occupational mobility between the two countries can be attributed to the greater amount of part-time employment and longer time away from work in Britain. Using the American coefficients, 70 per cent of the difference in downward mobility can be attributed to these two factors. The reason that it is possible to explain more of the difference using the British equations is that women who move into part-time work are more likely to move down the occupational scale in Britain than in the United States. In neither case do differences in occupational structure account for much of the difference.

Although these results highlight the importance of part-time employment and the length of time away from work as explanations of the downward occupational mobility that British women experience after having children, they do not explain why British women usually stay out longer than American women and are more likely to return to part-time employment. Lack of affordable child-care, difficulty in finding full-time employment, or preferences for staying at home with children are some of the possible explanations.

CONCLUSIONS

The gap between British and American women's occupational mobility experiences over their family formation phase is fairly large and it has not narrowed significantly between the generations. There appear to be more clerical jobs for women in the USA than in Britain, but in other respects the structure of women's employment in the two countries has some important similarities. It is all the more significant therefore that the majority of British women's experiences are worse than their American counterparts, although at the top of the occupational hierarchy the opposite is the case. These results suggest that women in higher-grade occupations in Britain can suffer less loss of status than women in the USA, but that the majority of British women in clerical occupations or below have more downward and less upward mobility over their family-formation period. British women also have far more part-time than full-time jobs and spend longer out of work than American women.

The advantages which American women have over British women as far as occupational mobility is concerned apply to both younger and older cohorts. Neither do these results suggest that any great improvement has been occurring between the generations of British women. In some cases there might have been a deterioration; for example, of the older women in clerical work before childbirth, 36 per cent had experienced downward occupational mobility in their most recent job in 1980 whereas the same proportion for younger British women was 40 per cent, and the older women had a slightly higher proportion with upward mobility. We have been examining the younger cohorts of women whilst they are still in the middle of their family formation phase, or have recently completed it. The older cohorts are further on from their family formation phase. It is interesting to note therefore that the results of the older women show a similar kind of picture of losses and gains over their family formation to that seen at its beginning in the younger group. One way of interpreting the differences between these generations is that the older women are further along the path which involves a recovery of any loss of status caused by childbirth. American women are again in a better position on the whole than British women in this respect.

The most striking difference is the movement of British women out of clerical, skilled and factory jobs and into less-skilled and lower-paid jobs after they have children, whereas women in the USA actually show a slight improvement in occupational status during this period. We have shown that higher levels of part-time employment and the longer period away from work both explain a great deal of the greater downward occupational mobility in Britain.

In seeking further explanations for the differences between British and American women we can offer some tentative possibilities. What contributes to more part-time work and longer breaks in employment in Britain? Probably both demand and supply factors are important; labour demand and supply may in turn be influenced by legislation. On the supply side, lack of affordable child-care may lock British women into longer durations out of work and into part-time jobs when they return. Tax deductions or credits for child care have made it somewhat easier for American women to pay for child care and take full-time jobs. It may also be the case that American women have more opportunities than British women for post-school training and education.

On the demand side, there appear to be more higher-grade non-manual and clerical jobs open to American women than to British women. It is possible that the earlier enactment and more aggressive enforcement of equal opportunities laws in the USA have contributed to this difference. Increasing the number of women in managerial and administrative jobs has probably been one of the major successes of this legislation. However, there is little reason to believe that equal opportunities legislation has created much clerical employment. Rather, demand in traditionally female clerical occupations has increased throughout the 1960s and 1970s at well above the rate of growth in employment in the economy as a whole. There is clearly a need for further analysis of these and other explanations for the differences between American and British women's experiences.

NOTES

1. See Jusenius (1976) for US definitions of 'typical' and 'atypical' occupations.
2. See Sandell and Shapiro (1978) and Corcoran and Duncan (1979) who

estimate that only 25–30 per cent of the gap can be accounted for by differences in work-history.

3.   For a description of logit regression analysis see Pindyke and Rubinfeld (1976).

4.   A study of American women by Long and Jones (1980) illustrated that the consequences of taking part-time work in the USA were serious and a deterioration in status frequently resulted.

5.   This technique has been widely used in research on wage differentials between men and women and between racial and ethnic groups (Blinder, 1973; Oaxaca, 1973; Corcoran and Duncan, 1979). A complete description of the method and some of its limitations may be found in Iams and Thornton (1975).

5 Industrial Mobility

INTRODUCTION

The counterpart to women's occupational classifications are their industrial classifications which have received relatively little attention in academic work even though the economic structure is most usually discussed in terms of the distribution of industries. Industries form the backbone structure of an economy, and determine to a large extent the range of occupations on offer. Women's employment changes of the post-war era have been clearly linked to industrial changes in the British and American economies. Notably, women's employment has increased in the growing services sector and in Britain the employment opportunities in the services sector have been largely part-time. If we are interested in the relationships between the structure of opportunities in the economy and women's employment experiences, therefore, we should not omit some consideration of the industrial categories of women's work.

In Britain women form a very high proportion (over 50 per cent) of the workforce of the clothing and footwear, distribution, banking and finance etc., professional and scientific services and miscellaneous services.[1] Women are distributed more evenly through the range of industries in Britain than through the range of occupations, but large proportions of women were in distribution (18 per cent) in 1971, professional and scientific services (22 per cent) and miscellaneous services (15 per cent). A similar pattern of women's distribution through the industrial structure can be seen in the USA.

Both Britain and the USA have been experiencing a similar set of industrial changes over the post-war era (and even before then). There have been decreases in manufacturing employment and increases in service employment and women's increasing labour-force participation has been clearly linked to the growth in services. Suffice it to say here that the same trends are visible both in Britain and the USA although the US economy has probably a higher proportion of services employment than is the case in Britain. There is no undisputed theory of why these changes have occurred, and in Britain the changes need to be considered in terms of the large growth in part-time women's work in services, a growth which is still occurring.[2]

OTHER STUDIES

Studies of women's industrial employment have taken place under three headings although two of them are interrelated. Women's employment has been a minor consideration in the debate about *de-industrialisation* in Britain, or the post-industrial society in the USA. The consideration of *the reserve army of labour* notion has examined women's distribution through the industrial employment structure, and *segmented labour market* discussions have also considered women's industrial employment. It is the concept of the reserve army of labour and the theory of segmented labour markets which are interrelated. We can review the conclusion of these three areas in turn below.

Deindustrialisation

The concept of de-industrialisation in Britain and the post-industrial society in the USA are descriptions of a process of industrial change which has been occurring for some time; namely, the decline of manufacturing and the rise of service industries.[3] This process has now reached the stage where services dominate industrial employment. In the USA this phenomenon is not seen as a serious problem partly because no external balance problems are created by the increase in services. There is some concern about the effects of de-industrialisation in the USA in so far as steel and automobiles – the big employers – are in decline. Also, the employment effects of multinational companies who move their manufacturing production to the developing countries to make use of cheap labour are being studied closely. On the whole, however, the growth of service industries has not been viewed as a major problem for the US economy. In Britain, however, economists have regarded these changes as having grave significance for the health of the British economy. The aspect of these changes which poses a problem largely arises because the open nature of the British economy means that a decline in manufacturing tends to create a balance-of-payments deficit in Britain (oil revenues are currently protecting Britain from a deficit).

The discussions of these sectoral changes have tended to neglect any consideration of the role of women's employment in these changes. The British and US discussions have at best merely noted in passing that women's increasing participation has been in the services growth sector. In Britain, the recognition of women's role came as part of a criticism of one of the earliest discussions of the problem. When the gender-based nature of the employment changes were noted it was clear that certain theories could not be correct.[4] Part of Bacon and Eltis's (1976) discussion of Britain's problems suggested that private sector employment (in manufacturing) was being crowded out by the growth of public sector employment. When the employment figures are disaggregated by sex as in Thatcher (1978), it becomes clear that the growth in public sector jobs in Britain was a growth in women's employment whereas the decline in manufacturing was a decline in men's employment. Since men's and women's employment are highly segregated and on the whole men are not prepared to do 'women's work' it is difficult to argue that women's employment increases in the public sector have crowded out men's manufacturing employment in Britain.

The discussions of industrial structure changes as far as aggregate employment effects are concerned leaves much to be desired. In addition, these discussions leave us with little understanding of the part which individual women play in the industrial structure and how this varies over their life cycle. One British study of the life-cycle variation of women's employment does exist, Sleeper (1975), but it was conducted at an aggregate level and so is particularly inappropriate to the nature of the task it set itself. Our analyses of these two surveys will provide more detail of life-cycle variations in women's industrial employment.

Reserve Army of labour

The concept of a reserve army of labour and the theory of segmented labour markets have shared the view that women are a marginal workforce. In the case of the reserve army idea, these workers are drawn into and displaced from the labour market according to the needs of capital over business-cycle fluctuations and changes in the industrial structure. The question of whether women fit the notion of a reserve army has been debated at a theoretical level and as an empirical issue.[5] The empirical work has taken place in Britain in the context of the growth of women's part-time employment in the service industries and the conclusions reached are that women's location in services has protected them from feeling the worst effects of recessions.[6] Several American studies reached similar conclusions.[7]

Segmented labour markets

The literature on segmented labour markets has also considered women's role in the industrial structure and the early American versions of the theory were not very explicit but they suggested that women would be found in marginal or secondary sector industries.[8] If one automatically describes service industries as marginal then clearly this generalisation would apply, but studies which have tried to offer more objective definitions of marginal industries have found that women are not wholly located in such industries, nor does this sort of terminology help us to understand the nature of women's employment.[9] Case-study material in Britain has supported this critique of segmented labour market theories and has tried to offer better formulations and a view of labour markets which build in the notion of organised struggle and workers' active resistance to replace more deterministic theories.[10]

Both the reserve army of labour notion and segmented labour market theories as well as the modifications to each are attempts to explain – at a macro or aggregate level – women's position in the industrial structure and how it has come about. They are still far from being a complete or full explanation of the changing nature of women's work, however, and they share with the discussions about de-industrialisation the neglect of what all this means for individual women over their life cycle of work. Starting from individual women's experiences may help to uncover more about the industrial structure of employment in a way that will be complementary to macro-level theories. It is to this concern that we shall now turn using the longitudinal data available from the WES and NLS sources.

INDUSTRIAL CLASSIFICATIONS

We were able to reclassify the US industrial categories in order to match them to the nine British ones, as was the case with occupational classifications. The broad nature of the British WES industrial categories which form the basis of our comparisons precludes a detailed analysis of structural variables which have been found to be important influences in women's employment participation in industries; for example we cannot examine the effects of levels of capital investment, productivity, firm size, market concentration or level of men's wages.[11] The classification does permit us to examine the much discussed divide between manufacturing and service industries around which the economic structure of our post-industrial economies are meant to revolve. The combination of insurance, a private sector industry and government into one category by WES unfortunately precluded any further comparisons of public-sector and private-sector employment.

INDUSTRIAL CHANGE OVER FAMILY FORMATION

In Chapter 2, we saw from a comparison of British and American women's most recent industrial classification that British women were more likely to be employed in manufacturing industries than were American women of the same age group. Whilst in the USA there was relatively little variation between the age cohorts in their distributions between manufacturing and services (although there were some differences between more finely divided categories) in Britain more of the older women were in manufacturing industries than was the case for the younger women. This change could be either a life-cycle effect or a result of structural change in the economy, or both.

A summary of the distributions by industry of the younger women in their last job before childbirth and their first job after is provided in Table 5.1. British women are far more likely than American women to be in manufacturing industries than on both sides of the break from work for childbirth. However, there are some differences in the changes which appear to be taking place. In Britain, textiles, engineering and other manufacturing industries all have lower proportions after childbirth than they did before. In the USA this finding is only significantly evident in engineering, the rest of the manufac-

TABLE 5.1   *Industrial distributions of younger women before and after childbirth (as percentages)*

Industry	Last job before childbirth		First job after childbirth	
	British	American	British	American
Food, drink, etc.	4.4	1.1	4.1	1.6
Textiles, clothing, etc.	10.9	4.5	7.6	4.1
Engineering	10.6	7.5	7.9	5.2
Other manufacturing	9.9	4.3	6.3	4.6
Distribution	19.7	20.2	15.5	22.8
Professional and scientific services	17.9	30.2	22.2	27.9
Insurance and government	11.4	13.7	8.9	13.8
Miscellaneous services	13.7	16.1	24.8	17.8
Primary production	1.5	2.3	2.7	2.1
Total %	100.0	100.0	100.0	100.0
N	842	1538	856	1538

SAMPLE   Women with children who have ever returned to work after childbirth.

turing industries either keeping similar proportions or even experiencing a slight increase. Whereas there appears to be a clear-cut shift out of manufacturing over childbirth in Britain, it is not so clearly the case in the USA.

The distribution industry has roughly similar proportions of the women's workforce in both Britain and the USA before childbirth – according to these figures approximately 20 per cent. After childbirth there is a larger gap between the countries since the British proportion declines to approximately 16 per cent and the American proportion increases to 23 per cent. Very few women are employed in the primary industries either in Britain or in the USA.

The USA has higher proportions of women in professional and scientific services, in insurance etc. and in miscellaneous services before childbirth than Britain. The total proportions for these three industries are 43 per cent for Britain and 64 per cent for the USA. Whereas in the USA the proportions in these three industries after childbirth are similar, totalling 60 per cent, in Britain the proportion increases greatly to 56 per cent especially in professional and scientific services and miscellaneous services. At this aggregate level, therefore, there appear to be significant shifts in British women's industrial employment either side of childbirth, but more stability at this time in the US women's industrial distributions. The transitions will permit us to see whether these impressions of greater British mobility are in fact accurate.

The summary of transitions between the last job before childbirth and the first job after are set out in Tables 5.2 and 5.3 for the British and American samples of younger women respectively. More disaggregated tables will be examined shortly. By considering manufacturing and service industries as a whole in the first instance we can see more clearly the broad structure of changes taking place. The size of the diagonal elements show that British women generally experience more industrial mobility at this time than the American women, and Britain's extra mobility is a flow out of manufacturing and distribution, but not services. British women tend to stay in manufacturing and distribution industries over their family formation less than American women, but in both countries there are large transitions out of manufacturing and into services at this time. Women who are already in services before childbirth are most likely to stay in this sector in both countries (78–9 per cent stay). Women in primary industries are amongst those least likely to stay in the same industry and they move into services after childbirth in Britain or into services and distribution in the USA. Women in primary industries are a very small group and there is hardly any inflow into these primary industries. The largest difference between British and American women is in the movement out of distribution which is far greater in Britain at this time.

The difference in industrial changes between the USA and Britain is not sufficiently great to provide an explanation of the difference in occupational mobility between the two countries. It is not necessarily the case that a move from manufacturing to services is automatically one involving downward occupational mobility although there is clearly an association of this kind in Britain. Service-sector employment in the USA, therefore, does not automatically mean jobs of lower status.

One important difference between the two countries visible along the bottom row of each matrix table lies in the proportions of return jobs in part-time work. The proportions of women in part-time work after childbirth are higher in Britain than in the USA in every industrial sector, and the gap is especially wide in manufacturing industries and services; in Britain 62 per cent of return jobs in manufacturing are part-time jobs whereas 15 per cent are part-time in the USA; in services 40 per cent of US jobs are part-time compared

TABLE 5.2 Summary of industrial changes between last job before first birth and first return job of younger British women (as percentages)

Last before child birth \ Return job	Manufacturing	Distribution	Services and government	Primary production	Total	N=	%
Manufacturing	46	13	37	4	100	302	35.8
Distribution	22	35	42	1	100	166	19.7
Services and government	10	11	79	1	100	363	43.0
Primary production	23	–	39	39	100	13	1.5
							100
Percentage of first return jobs in part time	62	63	77	70			844

SAMPLE   Women with at least one child who ever returned to work.

TABLE 5.3 *Summary of industrial changes between last job before first birth and first return job of younger American women*

(as percentages)

Last job before first birth \ Industry of first return job	Manufacturing	Distribution	Services and government	Primary production	Total	N=	%
Manufacturing	54	16	30	–	100	269	17.4
Distribution	11	54	33	2	100	310	20.2
Services and government	6	15	78	1	100	911	60.1
Primary production	15	22	24	39	100	48	2.3
Percentage working part-time at first job after	15	55	40	49	40	1538	100

SAMPLE Women who have had at least one childbirth and have ever returned after childbirth.

with 77 per cent in Britain. In Britain most part-time jobs are in services whereas in the USA distribution has the highest proportion of part-time jobs. An important difference occurs because as a major destination category after childbirth, the majority of British services jobs are part-time, but this is not the case for services in the USA.

The disaggregated industry transitions across childbirth are displayed in Tables 5.4 and 5.5 for younger British and American women. The greater mobility of British as compared with American women out of manufacturing industries over childbirth can be seen to apply to all the separate industries; the difference is most marked for the category of 'other manufacturing', and the two countries are not so different in the experiences of the food and textile industries. It is clear that the miscellaneous services industries consistently takes the highest inflow from those who leave manufacturing at this time in both countries, but especially so in Britain, although professional and scientific services also get large inflows from those who move out of manufacturing. Miscellaneous services and professional and scientific services, of course, have the highest proportions of part-time jobs in Britain, as the bottom row of Table 5.4 illustrates, so the industrial movement is linked to the move out of full-time into part-time work over childbirth.

Britain has a higher flow out of distribution at this time than the USA, but with the individual service industries, sometimes Britain, at other times the USA has the greater mobility. With miscellaneous services, Britain has a lower outflow than the USA, but for professional and scientific services the flow out is similar for the two countries. A substantial part of the outflow from individual service industries at this time is a flow into other services, especially in Britain. The disaggregate picture therefore shows that more industrial mobility takes place than appeared in the aggregate tables discussed earlier, but it is between service industries. It is not so common for industrial mobility to take place between manufacturing industries within the manufacturing sector. The relative lack of opportunities for part-time work in manufacturing undoubtedly explains women's drift towards, or their preference for, service employment after childbirth. It is clear that no US industry offers the same amount of part-time work to women as does the equivalent British industry and even British manufacturing industries which have fewer part-time workers than service industries in Britain still have more part-time employment than US services. It is clear that the structure of industrial employment for women is quite different in Britain and

TABLE 5.4 Industrial changes between last job before first birth and first return job of younger British women (as percentages)

Last job before childbirth	Food, drink, etc.	Textiles, Clothing	Engineering	Other manufacturing	Distribution	Professional and scientific services	Insurance and government	Miscellaneous services	Primary production	Total %	N =
Food, drink, etc.	27	3	8	–	16	19	3	19	5	100	37
Textiles, clothing	4	48	4	4	11	9	4	12	3	100	92
Engineering	1	3	30	5	15	8	11	24	3	100	89
Other manufacturing	8	4	6	24	11	16	5	24	4	100	84
Distribution	5	3	8	6	35	13	4	25	1	100	166
Professional and scientific services	–	–	3	1	6	70	6	13	1	100	151
Insurance and government	1	3	4	6	17	17	37	13	2	100	97
Miscellaneous services	2	4	4	2	11	10	4	61	2	100	115
Primary production	–	–	–	23	–	–	8	31	39	100	13
Percentage of first return jobs as part-time	64	58	58	63	63	76	66	83	70		844

SAMPLE Women with at least one chilbirth who have ever returned to work.

TABLE 5.5 Industrial change between last job before first birth and first return job of younger American women (as percentages)

Last job before childbirth	Food, drink, etc.	Textiles, clothing	Engineering	Other manufacturing	Distribution	Professional and scientific services	Insurance and government	Miscellaneous services	Primary production	Total %	N =
Food, drink, etc.	29	–	16	–	8	–	7	36	4	100	18
Textiles, clothing	2	51	4	6	11	7	7	13	–	100	73
Engineering	4	5	36	6	15	10	14	11	–	100	108
Other manufacturing	–	2	3	49	17	14	6	9	–	100	70
Distribution	1	3	4	4	54	12	7	13	2	100	310
Professional and scientific services	1	–	1	1	13	69	6	8	1	100	442
Insurance and government	2	1	2	3	17	11	52	10	2	100	203
Miscellaneous services	1	3	3	2	18	7	9	56	–	100	266
Primary production	1	4	3	6	22	18	5	2	39	100	48
Percent worked part-time at first job return	26	5	12	22	55	43	27	46	49	40	1538

SAMPLE   Women with at least one chilbirth who have ever returned to work.

TABLE 5.6 *Summary of industrial changes between last job before first birth and first return job of older British women (as percentages)*

Last job before childbirth	First return job						
	Manufacturing	Distribution	Services and government	Primary	Total	N=	%
Manufacturing	49	14	34	3	100	548	42.7
Distribution	10	44	43	2	100	209	16.3
Services & government	13	14	71	3	100	480	37.4
Primary	10	11	22	56	100	45	3.5
Percentage of first return jobs in part-time	52	73	70	70		100	
						1282	

SAMPLE   Women with at least one childbirth who have ever returned.

the USA therefore, with respect to the growth of women's part-time work.

The transition of older British women between the last job before and the first job after childbirth are displayed in Table 5.6. More of the older than younger British women are in manufacturing industries before childbirth, but their transition proportions are very similar; 48–9 per cent stay in manufacturing jobs across the first family-formation break; 34–7 per cent move from manufacturing to services and 71–9 per cent stay in services. There is therefore a large inflow into services in both age groups on the return to work. This comparison shows therefore that in Britain, the structural changes in the economy with a move towards services are reflected in the fact that more younger women are employed in services before childbirth, although these changes are not great. The biggest effect comes from a life-cycle effect experienced by both generations of women over their family-formation phase. The same phenomenon is visible in the USA.

CONCLUSIONS

There has been a tendency for structural changes in the British and American economies to be reflected in and rely upon women's break from work over family formation when major shifts occur out of manufacturing into services. The effect is less pronounced in the American data because there are not so many women employed in manufacturing industries in the USA. The implications of this shift for British and American women differ and British women experience more downward occupational mobility and less upward occupational mobility predominantly, we think, because service-sector jobs in Britain, but not in the USA, are largely part-time jobs. If British women are protected from the effects of recession by being in the growing service-sector, they gain that measure of employment security at the expense of their occupational status. There is some evidence that part-time work in the USA may not involve the same loss of occupational status which it often implies in Britain.

The structure of industry has accommodated to women's work in Britain to a far greater extent than it has in the USA, although this may be a mixed blessing. British women's movement out of manufacturing and into services over their break from work for childbirth is undoubtedly linked to their supply-side desire for part-time jobs whilst they are bearing the responsibilities of child-rearing. The tax considerations for child care in the USA which promote women's return to full-time work after childbirth mean that this preference for part-time work in the USA is not so great, neither is the shift out of manufacturing so pronounced. There are demand considerations however since in Britain this process has been occurring whilst men's employment in manufacturing has been declining. In this sense, the seemingly 'natural' turnover of women because of childbirth allows manufacturing industries in Britain to shed their workforce of women without any of the contractual problems which men present. It would not be surprising therefore to see manufacturing industries taking on younger women and maybe even preferring this group of workers to the extent that they may perhaps refuse to employ re-entrant women with children. At any rate, the changing industrial structure of the British economy is highly related to the changing structure of women's life-cycle employment. The comparison of British and American experiences in this respect allows us to see that the changing industrial structure is also highly related to the social, economic and legislative position of women in a country. We can see in these life-cycle changes of women the clear effects of child-care constraints in Britain promoting both a desire in women for part-time work and an accommodation to this cheap (and maybe vulnerable) labour force by industry. In comparison the American women experience less of a constraint over child care, and less of a desire for part-time work and industries have not bothered to provide part-time work in the USA. The power of social policies and their interrelationships with the industrial and occupational structures has been demonstrated again in this chapter.

NOTES

1. See Joseph (1983).
2. See Dex and Perry (1984).
3. For a discussion of the post-industrial society by an American writer see Bell (1974) and for a discussion of deindustrialisation in Britain see Blackaby (ed.) (1978) and Gershuny (1978).
4. See Thatcher (1978) in Blackaby (ed.) (1978).
5. See, for example, Beechey (1977) and Bruegel (1979).
6. See Bruegel (1979) and Dex and Perry (1984).
7. See Rosenfeld (1980).
8. For example, Piore (1975).
9. For example, Bridges (1980).
10. For example, Armstrong (1982).
11. See Bridges (1980) and Beck *et al.* (1978).

6 Conclusions

It is now time to return to the questions posed in the introduction; how have social policies and social structures affected women's working lives in the two countries? We are particularly interested in how equal opportunities policies and legislation are affecting women's experiences, whether child-care policies, tax and maternity benefit provisions play an important role and whether employment opportunities differ in Britain and the USA. These questions are considered in this chapter as part of our explanations for the major differences which we found between British and American women's experiences.

As a summary of our findings, we can point to both similarities and differences in the ways that women combine paid employment and childbearing in Britain and the USA. In both countries most women take time away from employment to take care of their children, and many return to work part-time after childbirth. However, British women spend more years out of the labour market and are much more likely to take part-time jobs than their American counterparts. In both countries the length of time spent at home after childbearing begins has decreased over the past twenty years.

In Britain a great deal of downward occupational mobility occurs when women return to work after childbirth. Many women move out of clerical and semi-skilled factory work into other kinds of semi-skilled and unskilled jobs, the great majority being part-time jobs. In the USA, there is much less downward occupational mobility and to a great extent the downward mobility of some women is offset by the upward mobility of others. In Britain there is much less upward mobility and the result is a decline in the average occupational status of women after children are born. The employment position of British women with children is therefore considerably worse than that of their American counterparts. In both countries women who work part-time are more likely than full-time workers to move downward in occupational status. In fact, we found that much of the difference in downward occupational mobility between the two countries could be attributed to the longer time British women are away from work and their greater propensity to work part-time after returning. The greater amount of upward mobility of American women tends to be associated with full-time employment as well.

We need to consider why there is a greater amount of part-time work in Britain, why women spend longer away from the labour market over childbirth in Britain, and why some American women experience upward occupational mobility at this time. There are three types of potential explanations for these differences; supply-side factors could be operating through women's preferences and the constraints they face; demand-side factors could be important, working through the structure of opportunities; and policies and legislation could be important parts of the explanations. Whilst we have listed these potential explanations as three alternatives they are not necessarily mutually exclusive and it would be surprising if social policies did not affect both supply and demand sides. In this sense policies and legislation can potentially have both direct and indirect effects on experiences.

The conclusions which we reach in the rest of this chapter are that policies have had direct and indirect effects on women's experiences in Britain and the USA but also supply- and demand-side factors have been influential. It is the coincidence of a number of elements which explains women's experiences and the differences between them in Britain and the USA since the mid-1960s. One could argue that supply-side changes in women's preferences for work must have preceded and caused the policy enactments which facilitated their working more. Meehan (1985) argues that this was not the case, however, particularly in the USA. We are more convinced therefore of the power certain policies have had in producing the changes we have found. The complicated nature of our conclusions will become visible as we consider explanations for the major areas of difference between British and American women.

PART-TIME WORK

In considering the link between downward occupational mobility and returning to work part-time after childbirth we can note that part-time work has this detrimental effect in both Britain and the USA. In this sense, there is something about the nature of part-time work which makes it likely to produce downward occupational mobility.

Part-time work must tend to be located more towards the bottom end of the occupational hierarchy in both countries. The fact that there was a much higher probability of experiencing downward mobility by going into part-time work in Britain is partly because there appear to be far more part-time jobs in Britain, but also that they are more likely than American part-time jobs to be low-skilled. In Britain the semi-skilled domestic and unskilled occupations were almost wholly part-time after childbirth and these were occupations into which many British women moved on their first return to work. It should be noted at this point that if women go into part-time jobs after childbirth then as a consequence they have a high probability, especially in Britain, of losing their occupational status. The situation could be improved if more part-time jobs became available in the higher-grade occupations, but there are still human capital effects from the loss of work experience which need to be considered.

We need to consider why there are more part-time jobs in Britain and why they predominate in certain occupations. On the supply side we think it is reasonable to suggest that British women have a greater preference than American women for part-time work. It is likely however that British women's preference for part-time work is related to the child-care constraints they face. If a woman wants to work after childbirth, in a context where women are seen as having primary responsibility for child-care, then taking a part-time job and relying on husbands or close relatives to look after the children whilst she is at work is one way of achieving the two objectives. This is an option which many women take in Britain, as we have found. In the USA the same problem is tackled knowing that at least some of any child-care expenses can be offset against tax. Not surprisingly we found that more American women chose to pay for child-care and work full time. We think that part of American women's greater preference for full-time work is the result of the favourable tax provisions for child-care expenses which have been operating in the USA. It is also the case that women get benefits from working full-time which they would not get from a part-time job. The most important of these is that most employers pay for health insurance for full-time employees in the USA, but few provide insurance for part-time workers. The escalating costs of health care in the USA make this a valuable benefit. Clearly, it is not an incentive to British women to work full-time as they receive health care free. In this way the social-policy provisions in the two countries are having an indirect effect on women's occupational status. Since far more American women are single parents, there are also greater financial pressures on them which act as an incentive to choose full-time work.

In our comparison of attitudes towards work and home we found that British and American women were very similar. However, it could well be that British women with children think of part-time employment but not full-time employment as socially acceptable, whereas American women may find either part or full-time employment acceptable.

British women's preference for part-time work cannot be the whole reason for Britain having more part-time jobs however. We saw in the first chapter that there are favourable conditions of employment for British employers who take on part-time workers and this demand-side consideration has undoubtedly played some part in creating part-time opportunities in Britain. Martin and Roberts' analysis (1984) of the women and employment survey found that the hours worked by part-time women peaked just below the 16 hours after which employees are eligible for greater employment protection in law and probably more fringe benefits from their employers. Case studies of British firms and industries confirm that some employers have switched to employing more part-time employees to benefit from these provisions (Robinson and Wallace, 1984), although there are additional overhead and recruitment costs to employing part-timers, especially when the nature of the work does not require part-time employees. In the USA where there are no off-setting tax advantages, these additional costs are probably sufficiently great to dissuade US employers from offering much part-time work. Far more of the part-time jobs in Britain are in low-skilled, often public-sector jobs where the nature of the work appears to demand a part-time commitment; for example, cleaners, dinner ladies, home helps, etc. In these cases the greater number of part-time jobs in Britain is partly linked to Britain's welfare state. There is no reason, however, to think that the USA has any less need for some of these jobs. We suspect that jobs like part-time cleaning and to a lesser extent part-time clerical or secretarial jobs are not part-time jobs to the same extent in the USA as they are in Britain because in the USA, far more contract agencies have grown up. These offer employers part-time employment, but offer workers full-time employment. There are a set of demand-side considerations which make part-time work more preferable in Britain. They are brought about by a mixture of policy differences and private initiatives, and they contribute, mostly indirectly, to British women's greater downward occupational mobility.

It is worth noting that the legislation outlawing discrimination in employment against women does not so obviously apply to part-time employment; the contractual position of part-time workers is often very much weaker than for full-time workers so that equal opportunities legislation offers them fewer benefits. Some recent British court cases have served to strengthen the position of part-time employees, particularly with respect to redundancy (Robinson and Wallace, 1984). In so far as women are the predominant holders of part-time jobs they are less likely to be discriminated against in recruitment to these jobs and men are not so concerned to compete for lower-skilled jobs. We cannot attribute the downward occupational mobility which is caused by women returning to part-time jobs to differences in discrimination legislation in the two countries in any direct way, therefore, although the potential benefits from equal opportunities legislation are much weaker in Britain than in the USA by virtue of women's greater predominance in part-time work. An increase in the availability of part-time jobs in the higher-grade occupations would not necessarily improve women's security under law, although clearly it would improve their status and rewards.

We do think, however, that there might well be an environmental effect from the more aggressive pursuit of equal opportunities for American women. This environmental effect appears to have opened up more opportunities to American women and it has raised their overall status in the eyes of employers. By contrast, in Britain, employers probably see women much more as a part-time and marginal workforce who are suitable for lower-skilled 'women's' jobs and who are in fact not protected by legislation to the same extent as full-time workers especially if they work fewer than 16 hours. We think that there is probably an indirect effect of the legislation in the two countries on women's occupational status. If this environmental effect operates, British women's position could be improved by a more aggressive pursuit of equal opportunities for women and by the introduction of the US type of class action suits. Indeed, unless women's status is more visibly protected through court cases against large British employers we cannot see that employers will change their view of women as marginal and disposable workers.

TIME OUT OF EMPLOYMENT

The most likely explanations for the large differences we found in the duration of time women spend out of employment are the social-policy differences in the two countries and supply-side differences. These differences appear to be less related to either structural differences in employment opportunities in the two countries or to other demand-side considerations. British women appeared to have an advantage in social-policy provisions from the statutory maternity leave provisions, but in practice, only a minority of women benefited. In the USA in contrast, although there is no statutory provision, nearly 50 per cent of younger women reported having some private maternity leave schemes. The results of the two countries support the idea that maternity-leave provisions, whether statutory or private, play a large role in reducing the time out of work for childbirth. Obviously such provisions also protect women's occupational status at this time, so long as they are prepared to work full-time. It is likely that in the future maternity-leave provisions in Britain will go some way towards eliminating the differences between American and British women. It is likely that more women would benefit from maternity-leave provisions in Britain if these provisions included the opportunity to return, in the first instance, to a part-time job. This would be a way of improving British women's status without there necessarily being any other changes for example in child-care provision.

The other aspect of policy provisions which has obvious relevance to women's timing of their return to work is that of child care. The tax provisions for child-care expenses in the USA mean that there are fewer constraints on American women's decision to return to work. It is therefore not surprising to see them making that return faster than British women. Our results also suggest that women's position in the British labour market would change quite markedly if child-care expenses could be reduced through tax deductions.

UPWARD OCCUPATIONAL MOBILITY

As we have shown, many women maintain their previous occupational status after having children. Some women even manage to move upward in occupational status at this stage, but upward occupational mobility is much more common in the USA than in Britain. We have suggested that part of the difference in upward mobility between the two countries is due to the greater amount of part-time employment in Britain. Probably few part-time jobs offer the kinds of work experience or on-the-job training that helps some women obtain better jobs. The greater gaps in the work experience of British women would also make it less likely that they would have acquired skills that would help them to obtain higher status jobs.

One of the areas in which equal opportunities legislation has had an impact in the USA is in opening-up administrative and managerial jobs to women. Movement into these jobs is not common in the period immediately after childbearing begins, but as their children grow older many women have moved into managerial and administrative jobs. To a lesser extent, movement into skilled manual jobs has also been aided by this legislation. However, much of the upward mobility that we saw in the US data was movement from sales and semi-skilled jobs into the clerical occupations. Since clerical work is predominantly female in any event, it does not appear likely that legislation has had a direct impact on the movement of young mothers into this work. (Indirectly, some clerical jobs may have opened up through some women being promoted out of them into administrative positions.) A more important part of the explanation of the upward mobility into clerical occupations in the USA is probably to be found in the rapid expansion in the demand for clerical workers over almost the entire post-war period in the USA. Therefore, opportunities for clerical employment have been plentiful.

On the supply side, probably a majority of American women who do not plan to attend college acquire some clerical skills while in high school, so a great many women are either already qualified for clerical jobs or can become so without extensive training. Clerical courses for adults are widely available in night schools, junior colleges and business schools. More widely available opportunities for further education and training may also explain the greater amount of movement of women into intermediate non-manual jobs in the USA. Our data sets did not have the necessary information to allow us to test this hypothesis directly, so our evidence must be somewhat impressionistic at present. American colleges and universities are actively recruiting 'non-traditional' students, especially women aged 25 or older, in order to make up for declining enrolments as the number of young people in the usual college age-range declines. In 1978, over 33 per cent of the students in American colleges and universities were in this older age-range, and well over 50 per cent of these older students were women (National Center for Education

Statistics, 1980). Between 1967 and 1982 about 4 per cent of the older cohort of NLS women received college degrees; all of these women were at least 30 years old and many were much older, Morgan (forthcoming). Much larger numbers took short courses or enrolled in vocational training courses. Most of this education appears to have been oriented toward improvement of employment prospects (Shaw and O'Brien, 1983; Shaw, 1984). Among younger American women, returning to college (or entering for the first time) after a period spent at home must be even more common.

Another factor that should be mentioned is that, because of more widespread automobile ownership in the USA, American women can seek work and make child-care arrangements at a greater distance from home than can their British counterparts. About half the women in the NLS reported that their families owned two or more automobiles, and nearly 90 per cent owned at least one. It has been estimated that about 70 per cent of adult women in the USA have a driver's licence, and the percentage must be even higher among women in the child-rearing years since many older women do not drive. Being able to drive a considerable distance to work frees American women from having to take nearby jobs that offer little except convenience. They can therefore be more selective in the kinds of jobs they choose.

POLICIES

A series of policy implications follow from our analysis. Some of these have been noted already but they can be assembled here alongside other alternatives for improving women's employment prospects in Britain and the USA. In that British women's employment position was found to be worse than that of American women because of part-time work and longer spells out of employment, we might be tempted to advocate more full-time employment and shorter durations out of work for British women. We prefer, however, to allow women to choose the mix of working and domestic responsibilities they desire and our policy suggestions are therefore directed at reducing the constraints women face in making their choices.

Women's position could be improved in both countries if part-time work did not deny women security and other benefits such as health care in the USA. Improving the status of part-time jobs in this way would seem to imply additional costs to employers, as things stand.

However, innovations such as flexible benefit plans, which some employers have begun to offer in the USA might well be able to improve the status of part-time jobs without significantly increasing employers' costs. Flexible-benefit schemes allow workers to choose within a given cost constraint the package of fringe benefits which best suits them. For example, they can trade-off holidays for sick pay or health insurance, etc. Schemes like these have been introduced in the USA, perhaps in part because employers are concerned about their image as a 'good employer'. The promotion of the value of 'good employers' would be of benefit to women and workers generally in Britain. We feel Britain lags behind the USA in this respect. The availability of part-time jobs is only likely to increase in the USA if employers' insurance contributions were not greater for two part-time jobs than for one equivalent full-time job.

Women's employment prospects in Britain could also be improved by part-time jobs becoming more available in the higher-grade (non-manual) jobs. As things stand, women who want to work part-time in Britain are often forced to take up very low status jobs. Furthermore, the USA has shown that not all jobs considered part-time in Britain need necessarily be part-time. It is possible for agencies to act in an intermediary fashion to provide workers with full-time jobs whilst providing customers with part-time services to a far greater extent than occurs at present in Britain. The increased use of agencies offering part-time services could improve the status of some 'women's' jobs in Britain.

The environment in which women are seeking jobs and returning to work could be improved in Britain if cases of sex discrimination were taken more seriously. If proven cases of sex discrimination could be given more publicity, if greater penalties and damages could be awarded and if employers came to regard sex discrimination as bad employment practice, British women's prospects would receive many indirect benefits.

Offering women tax deductions for child care would enable them to choose more freely whether they want to work full-time and pay for child care or work part-time and rely on relatives. British women would clearly benefit most by the introduction of such a scheme, but clearly American women could benefit by an improvement in the conditions of their scheme. A concomitant of such a policy in Britain might be that paid child-care services would need to increase.

Maternity leave provisions have undoubtedly improved women's prospects and we expect that the full extent of the improvement has yet to be seen, especially in Britain. American women could benefit from having more standardised and statutory provisions. In Britain, the right to return to a part-time job for a certain period would be very beneficial to women, as would the opportunity to take longer periods of unpaid leave without any loss of status.

American women's employment opportunities have been better over our period of interest partly because of a greater expansion of clerical work. The conclusion we derive from this finding – and we know it is commonly the case – is that growth in the economy is a way of boosting women's job prospects. Times of increased demand are almost bound to improve women's prospects more than times of recession, and social goals are easier to pursue through times of high demand. We do not wish to advocate growth as an alternative to other policies, however; nor do we accept that women's position cannot change without a background of economic growth. Effective changes will depend upon a will to enact them, although clearly some conditions provide a more favourable climate than others.

Appendix A   Data Sources and Technical Details

We will describe the main characteristics of the British Women and Employment Survey (WES) and the US National Longitudinal Surveys (NLS) in this appendix and then draw together the adjustments which were carried out to each data source in order to make direct comparisons between them.

THE WOMEN AND EMPLOYMENT SURVEY (WES)

The Women and Employment Survey consisted of a single interview between April and June of 1980 with each of 5588 women between the ages of 16 and 59. The sample was obtained by approaching a national random sample of addresses and interviewing all the women at each address. The sample details and response rates, etc., are described in Martin and Roberts (1984, ch. 1). The main interview schedule collected information about the women's education, training and current employment status, their family and household circumstances, their husbands' education and employment status, their attitudes and their work-history experience over the previous two years. In addition a work-history schedule was administered to most of these women (5320) which recorded systematically, on the basis of a memory recall, their working and not-working periods after leaving school (with dates) up to the interview. It has become usual in social sciences to use the term 'work' to refer to activity which may or may not be paid, with 'employment' being used to signify paid work. The WES survey used the term work in its everyday sense to mean paid work, for reasons given in Martin and Roberts (1984, ch. 1), and the same terminology is used here.

The analysis undertaken and reported in this book concentrates on using the information in the work-history schedule in conjunction with some of the information contained in the main schedule of the WES data.

Women in the sample were asked to give an outline structure of their work history from leaving full-time education onwards, in terms of periods of working full-time, working part-time, not working, and being in full-time education. The dates at which transitions took place between any of these types of activities was recorded. For purposes of the WES survey 'a period' had to span the duration of at least one month in order to be recorded. Working periods and not-working periods are therefore recorded to the nearest month. The interviewer was told to return, after outlining this basic structure, to the beginning of the work history and ask for further details about each period.

When the period was one of full- or part-time work women were asked about the jobs they had held within a working period and the occupation, the industry, whether or not they were a supervisor, their reason for leaving and the duration of each job were recorded. The most important feature to grasp about this procedure is that a 'working period' is one in which a number of jobs can be held and it could even cover experiences of unemployment so long as they lasted less than one month. A restricted range of twelve occupational and nine industrial classifications was used to classify women's jobs.

In the case of a period not-working, women were asked about their reasons and also their main reason for not working over the whole period. These reasons provide some information as to whether women were economically active, although not working, but no attempt was made to classify 'not working' periods, according to whether they were economically active or not. When a woman had started work again, at the end of the period of not working, she was asked why she had re-started work. Women were presented with a range of pre-coded answers in each case, and these had been determined after the pilot stage of the survey.

This systematic recording of working and not-working periods was combined with a series of life events of these women recorded in the main interview schedule. In particular, it was possible to see women's working activity alongside their marriage dates, the births of their children, adoptions or deaths of children, and the ends of their marriages (that is, by death or divorce). This mixture of life events, working and not-working experiences, reasons for leaving jobs and reasons for not working provided a very rich data source about these women's longitudinal experiences. The fact that this information was based on women's memories may raise certain questions about its accuracy. The OPCS/DE Report of this survey (Martin and Roberts, 1984) discusses this issue and provides reassuring details about the tests which were carried out. There is cross-checking information contained in questions within the interview schedule. Their warning does apply however; 'some caution should be attached to the inter- pretation of retrospective information' (Martin and Roberts, 1984).

THE NATIONAL LONGITUDINAL SURVEYS (NLS)

In the late 1960s the Employment and Training Administration of the US Department of Labor initiated the National Longitudinal Surveys of Work Experience (NLS) in which a sample of women and men in four different age groups were to be interviewed at one or two-year intervals over a five-year period. Subsequently the surveys were extended to fifteen years and in 1978 a new survey of youth, both male and female, was begun. Contents of the questionnaires, reports on results, and maintenance of data tapes and documentation for public use are the responsibility of the Center for Human Resource Research at the Ohio State University. Interviewing and initial data processing are performed by the US Bureau of the Census for the original four cohorts and by the National Opinion Research Center at the University of Chicago for the youth survey.

In this book we use the two earlier NLS women's cohorts, but do not include the women from the more recent youth cohort. The original NLS sample of mature women consisted of 5083 women chosen to be representative of all non-institutionalised, civilian women aged 30–44 living in the continental United States at the time of the first interview in 1967. By 1979 – the date of the last interview used in this report – 3812 women remained in the sample. The survey of young women, chosen in the same way, initially interviewed 5159 women who were aged 14–24 at the first interview in 1968. By 1980, 3801 of these women remained in the sample. In both surveys black women were over-sampled to provide sufficiently large numbers for separate analysis. In order to provide data which accurately represent the entire population, each sample case can be weighted by the inverse of its probability of falling into the sample. This procedure has been followed in the analysis presented in this book.

In any continuing survey, a major concern is whether the sample remains representative as people are lost to the survey because they cannot be located or refuse to be interviewed. Studies of the factors affecting attrition in the NLS have found little evidence of attrition bias on most measurable characteristics (Rhoton, 1984). One exception is that white respondents are slightly more likely to continue in the surveys than are black respondents. At each survey, we have adjusted the sampling weights to reflect differences in the probability that an individual would be interviewed in that particular year.

PROBLEMS IN MAKING COMPARISONS USING THE NLS AND WES

Since the WES depends on retrospective work histories, in some cases extending back for many years, while the NLS data on work experiences were collected over one- or two-year periods, we were concerned that differences which we found might be partially due to these differing methods of data collection. In particular, it seemed probable that very short periods of employment would be more easily overlooked if they had occurred in the more distant past.

Several factors make us confident that the differences in methods of data collection are not a major source of the differences we found in women's work experiences in the two countries. First, both data sets have been compared with other data sources in the two countries and neither appears to be seriously biased. Second, differences in work and occupational status at the time of the 1980 interviews in both countries, when no differences in recall are involved, parallel those found for other years when the data was retrospective in the WES but contemporaneous in the NLS. In addition, NLS data for older women for the years before the 1967 interview also depend on retrospective questions, so this source of difference will be less important for this group. Finally, the differences are sufficiently striking for it to be unlikely that our general conclusions would be altered by small differences in the accuracy of reporting caused by the greater 'recall' period in the British data.

COMPARING THE SURVEYS

In order to carry out direct comparisons between these British and US data adjustments to each data source were required.

1. Equivalent British cohorts

Equivalent British cohorts had to be obtained from the WES which matched the US cohorts by age. We refer to the two cohorts as *younger women* – women aged 14–24 on 1 January 1968. (These women would have been between the ages of 26 and 36 in 1980), and *older women* – women aged between 30 and 44 in May 1966. (These women would have been between the ages of 44 and 58 in 1980).

The numbers in the equivalent British cohorts were smaller than the US cohort. The total figures are displayed in Table A1. On occasions we have split each cohort into five-year sub samples. The sizes of these five-year sub-cohorts are also displayed in Table A1. The US sample sizes are smaller than the initial sample sizes because of attrition suffered in longitudinal surveys. The British data do not change in size because the work history was collected by recall, but the working experiences of these British women in the past are not necessarily representative of British women at that time.

2. Differences in the information collected in the two surveys

When the mature women's sample of the NLS were first interviewed in 1967 at ages 30–44, they were asked summary questions about their previous work experience, but complete work-histories were not attempted. Fortunately, for our cross-country comparison, the date of first working after the birth of the first child was one of the retrospective questions asked, but the occupation and industry of this job were not ascertained. Although information on the last job before first birth was not asked, the occupation and industry of the longest job held between school and marriage and the longest job held after marriage and before the first birth were both recorded. Whenever a longest job was reported between marriage and first birth, this job is assumed to be the last job before the first birth; otherwise the longest job between school and marriage is counted as the last job before the first birth. Since the average time between school-leaving and childbearing was about five years, these longest jobs were undoubtedly in many cases the actual last job before childbearing began, and in other cases should be reasonably representative of the kinds of jobs held by these women before they had children.

TABLE A1   *Total sample sizes of data sources in mid-1980*

	Younger women		Older women	
	British	American	British	American
Total	1423	3509	1705	3538
Five year age cohorts				
Born				
April 1922–March 1926			584	1069
April 1926–March 1931			567	1279
April 1931–March 1936			554	1190
January 1944–December 1948	726	1606		
January 1949–December 1953	697	1905		

From 1967 onward the amount of work information for the mature women varied, depending on the type of interview. In most years when interviews were conducted in person, detailed work histories since the previous interview were obtained (1971, 1972 and 1977). In years when shorter interviews were obtained by telephone (1968, 1969, 1974, 1976 and 1979) detailed information was obtained concerning current or most recent job, including starting and ending dates, occupation, industry, wages, and hours of work, but no information was obtained on other jobs held since the previous interview. However, the total number of weeks worked since the last interview was ascertained. For women whose first employment after childbearing occurred in one of the years without a detailed work history, it was necessary to estimate the approximate date of first return, based on total weeks worked between interviews. In all such cases, the latest date consistent with number of weeks worked and the date the current or most recent job began were used to estimate the length of time from the birth of the first child until the first return. To make the data more comparable with the WES, jobs lasting less than four weeks were not included when determining the date of

first employment after childbearing began. The occupation and industry of the current or most recent job were considered to be the
first occupation and industry after returning.

In the young women's sample a question was not asked in 1968 on
the first job held after the birth of the first child. Probably because
most of the sample had no children at this date, the need to obtain
this information for the small group of women who did have children
was not realised. Similarly, information was not always obtained on
the last job held before the birth of the first child when that birth
occurred prior to 1967. For this reason, only women who had their
first child in 1967 or later can be included in our analysis.

The general structure of the young women's interviews resembles
those of the older women. Detailed work histories were obtained in
1970, 1971, 1972, 1973 and 1978, and information on the current or
most recent job as well as total weeks worked was obtained in 1968,
1969, 1975, 1977 and 1980. Decision rules for determining the first
date of return and the first job after returning were the same as those
described for older women who first returned to work after 1967. The
occupation and industry of the last job before the first birth was
generally taken to be the current or most recent job held at the last
interview before the first birth.

3. Cohort comparability

The definitions of younger and older women are set by the limits of
the US cohorts as described in points (1) and (2) above. As mentioned already, younger American women who had their first child
before 1967 could not be included in the analysis. This meant that
women at the upper end of the younger cohort's age-range were
often excluded if they had their children at young ages. In order to
test whether this exclusion caused our results to be biased, the
analysis was repeated on a restricted group of British and American
younger women. Women who were over 33 in 1980 were excluded
from the whole younger women's samples. To all intents and purposes the restriction excludes from the younger cohort women whose
first child was born prior to 1967. This restriction made the British
and US cohorts more directly comparable. The restricted tables of
results were then compared with the whole samples. These additional
tables on the restricted samples are not provided because no significant biases were found.

4. Occupational and industrial classifications

The US occupational classification was very detailed and this permitted US occupations to be reclassified into the twelve much broader British WES occupational categories. This reclassification was carried out with the help of the OPCS. The full details are available from the authors. US industry categories were similarly reclassified into the nine WES industrial categories.

5. Definition of part-time work

Definitions of part-time work differ in Britain and the USA. In Britain, part-time work is generally defined as 30 hours or less whereas in the USA the standard definition is less than 35 hours. The US data contained the precise number of hours worked at each interview so that the US hours of work could be reclassified using the British definition of part-time. Where the British WES work history data are used, women were asked to define themselves as working either part- or full-time so that the British data are not so precisely defined in terms of hours worked. An analysis of the hours-worked distributions was undertaken from the precise figures available from interviews in 1979 or 1980 in the USA and Britain respectively. The differences found between British and American women with respect to the proportions in part-time work were independent of the definition used; far more British women were in part-time work on both British and US definitions of part-time work. We have adopted the British definition in all of our analysis since this definition coincides with the modality of the hours-distributions of both countries.

6. Comparing other variables

It was possible to get approximate comparability on other variables. In some cases, exactly the same questions were asked in both the American and British data, for example, attitudes. It was not possible or appropriate to adjust educational qualification differences in the two countries, so that education differences are measured in a way that is unique to each country. We are regarding the British O-level passes to be approximately equivalent to a High School Certificate in the USA.

Appendix B   Additional Tables

TABLE B1   *Employment rates of younger women's cohort at selected dates*
(as percentages)

British working	1968	1969	1970	1971	1972	1973	1975	1977	1978	1980
Full-time	58.0	57.6	54.4	50.2	44.6	40.1	33.2	28.2	26.6	24.9
Part-time	6.0	5.5	7.3	8.0	8.4	10.0	15.5	22.0	25.8	32.5
Total %	64.0	63.1	61.7	58.2	53.0	50.1	48.7	50.2	52.4	57.4
American working										
Full-time	22.1	26.9	32.3	35.2	39.6	43.7	45.6	45.9	47.1	49.7
Part-time	17.0	18.0	16.3	15.6	13.8	12.5	12.3	13.3	13.4	14.6
Total %	39.1	44.9	48.6	50.8	53.4	56.2	57.9	59.2	60.5	64.3

TABLE B2   *Employment rates of older women's cohort at selected dates*
(as percentages)

British working	1967	1969	1971	1972	1974	1976	1977	1979
Full-time	25.1	27.0	28.8	29.0	32.5	32.8	32.8	31.7
Part-time	19.4	21.9	25.6	27.6	30.7	33.3	33.7	35.0
Total %	44.5	48.9	54.4	56.6	63.2	66.1	66.5	66.7
American working								
Full-time	36.3	38.8	40.4	40.2	41.2	41.6	42.7	43.4
Part-time	9.9	11.2	12.4	12.8	14.3	13.2	14.2	13.9
Total %	46.2	50.0	52.8	53.0	55.5	54.8	56.9	57.3

TABLE B3 *Number of years not working between first birth and first return of younger women (as percentages)*

Not-working time in years	Returned at least once after childbirth		Including those who never returned since childbirth	
	British	*American*	*British*	*American*
0–11 mths	29.8	56.5	22.5	48.6
1–2 yrs	12.8	16.4	12.0	15.3
2–3	10.9	8.6	10.0	8.4
3–4	9.1	5.2	9.8	5.8
4–5	7.1	4.2	7.4	4.7
5–6	7.9	2.9	8.0	3.6
6–7	7.1	2.2	8.2	3.7
7–8	5.4	0.8	6.6	2.0
8–9	4.1	1.2	6.2	2.5
9–10	2.4	0.8	3.5	2.0
10–11	2.1	0.7	3.1	1.3
11–12	1.1	0.4	2.3	1.1
12–13	0.3	0.1	0.3	0.8
13 +	–	–	0.1	0.1
Total %	100.0	100.0	100.0	100.0
N =	634	1765	938	2112

SAMPLE Women with at least one childbirth.

TABLE B4   *Number of years not working between first birth and first return of older women (as percentages)*

Not-working time in years	Returned at least once after childbirth		Including those who never returned since childbirth	
	British	*American*	*British*	*American*
0–11 mths	12.6	25.2	11.0	22.8
1– 2 yrs	5.5	10.0	4.8	9.1
2– 3	6.3	5.8	5.6	5.2
3– 4	4.8	4.8	4.2	4.3
4– 5	4.8	3.3	4.2	3.0
5– 6	5.3	2.8	4.7	2.5
6– 7	5.5	3.5	4.8	3.2
7– 8	5.8	3.0	5.2	2.7
8– 9	4.9	3.2	4.5	2.9
9–10	5.8	3.3	5.3	3.0
10–11	5.1	3.5	4.5	3.1
11–12	5.5	3.3	4.9	3.0
12–13	0.9	3.4	0.8	3.1
13–14	4.3	3.1	3.9	3.0
14–15	4.4	3.3	4.0	3.2
15 +	18.3	18.5	27.6	25.9
Total %	100.0	100.0	100.0	100.0
N =	1200	2810	1368	3070

SAMPLE   Women with at least one childbirth

TABLE B5 *Means and standard deviations of variables*
(Standard deviations in parentheses)

	Younger women				Older women			
	British		American		British		American	
Variable								
LENG	4.27	(3.6)	1.57	(2.2)	8.48	(5.3)	7.72	(7.2)
YAGE	3.09	(2.4)	1.15	(1.5)	6.12	(4.3)	4.35	(4.6)
TREND	5.09	(2.7)	6.18	(2.5)	8.23	(4.4)	7.77	(4.0)
PROF	0.01	(0.1)	0.01	(0.1)	0.01	(0.04)	0.003	(0.0)
TEACH	0.04	(0.2)	0.08	(0.3)	0.03	(0.2)	0.04	(0.2)
NURS	0.07	(0.3)	0.07	(0.3)	0.04	(0.2)	0.04	(0.2)
INTE	0.02	(0.1)	0.04	(0.2)	0.01	(0.1)	0.02	(0.1)
CLER	0.19	(0.4)	0.34	(0.5)	0.18	(0.4)	0.34	(0.5)
SKIL	0.07	(0.3)	0.05	(0.2)	0.06	(0.2)	0.04	(0.2)
SEMF	0.18	(0.4)	0.09	(0.3)	0.20	(0.4)	0.12	(0.3)
QUAL1	0.15	(0.4)	—		0.11	(0.3)	—	
QUAL2	0.18	(0.4)	—		0.10	(0.3)	—	
NOTHS	—		0.16	(0.4)	—		0.33	(0.5)
MATL	0.04	(0.2)	—		0.02	(0.1)	—	
WORK	5.92	(3.2)	3.16	(2.7)	8.65	(4.0)	3.34	(3.5)
MTIME	1.83	(2.4)	2.28	(2.4)	2.59	(2.8)	2.11	(2.4)
HOME	2.16	(1.3)	2.16	(1.1)	2.57	(1.4)	2.57	(1.1)
YCHILD	3.17	(0.8)	2.79	(1.2)	—		—	
SCHILD	—		—		2.67	(0.8)	3.47	(1.6)
HUSB	0.19	(0.4)	2.61	(1.2)	0.20	(0.4)	2.71	(1.1)
FAMINC	3.21	(1.3)	13.71	(10.9)	2.94	(1.3)	11.73	(11.3)
NOLDCH	0.57	(0.7)	0.21	(0.5)	0.97	(1.2)	1.34	(1.9)
RACE	—		0.14	(0.5)	—		0.10	(0.4)
N =	770		1364		1147		2217	

TABLE B6 *First occupations of those younger British women included in, and excluded from, the analysis of occupational mobility (as percentages)*

Occupation of first job	Women with child who have ever returned (included in analysis)	Women with no children, or have not yet returned after childbirth (excluded from analysis)
Professional	0.7	1.6
Teacher	4.5	10.4
Nurse	4.6	6.5
Intermediate non-manual	1.7	2.5
Clerical	33.3	42.6
Sales	18.0	12.6
Skilled	10.0	8.8
Child care	1.6	1.3
Semi-skilled factory	17.9	9.5
Semi-skilled domestic	2.4	2.3
Other semi-skilled	3.9	1.3
Unskilled	1.2	0.5
Total %	100.0	100.0
N =	861	556

TABLE B7   *Summary of percentages of occupational mobility of younger women from last job before childbirth to first return job (as percentages)*

Occupation of last job before childbirth	First return job			
	Downward mobility		Upward mobility	
	British	*American*	*British*	*American*
Professional	(20)	(27)	–	–
Teacher	17	30	–	2
Nurse	26	10	2	–
Intermediate non-manual	(42)	51	8	18
Clerical	48	28	5	7
Skilled	42	27	9	19
Semi-skilled factory	43	25	5	20
Sales**	–	–	13	55
Child care**	–	–	(25)	43
Semi-skilled domestic**	–	–	29	47
Other semi-skilled**	–	–	28	34
Unskilled**	–	–	(17)	50

SAMPLE   Women with at least one childbirth who have ever returned to work.

()   Based on very small cell-sizes

**   Upward mobility consists of moving up to any of the jobs in the first group; semi-skilled factory or above.

TABLE B8 *Summary of percentages of occupational mobility for older women from last job before childbirth to most recent job (as percentages)*

Last job before childbirth	Downward mobility		Upward mobility	
	British	American	British	American
Professional	(0)	88	–	–
Teacher	19	33	–	2
Nurse	30	34	7	7
Intermediate non-manual	49	62	23	17
Clerical	32	23	11	19
Skilled	47	40	22	33
Semi-skilled factory	50	27	15	40
Sales*	–	–	37	61
Child care*	–	–	33	65
Semi-skilled domestic*	–	–	39	55
Other semi-skilled*	–	–	31	51
Unskilled*	–	–	28	57

SAMPLE Women with at least one childbirth who have ever returned.

* Upward mobility consists in moving to any of jobs in first group; semi-skilled factory or above.

() Based on very small cell sizes.

TABLE B9 *Means of variables in downward occupational mobility regressions of younger women (as percentages)*

Variable	British	American
DOWN	0.410	0.261
PART	0.705	0.404
TIME	3.690	1.465
OCC1	0.066	0.122
OCC2	0.084	0.112
OCC3	0.034	0.050
OCC4	0.425	0.513
OCC5	0.112	0.064
N =	678	1024

TABLE B10 *Logit coefficients (unadjusted) from regressions on downward occupational mobility*

	British		American	
PART	1.267	(6.1)	0.815	(5.3)
TIME	0.117	(4.9)	0.128	(3.9)
OCC1	−1.087	(2.5)	0.006	(0.0)
OCC2	−0.531	(1.5)	−1.149	(2.9)
OCC3	0.179	(0.4)	1.131	(3.3)
OCC4	0.126	(0.6)	−0.109	(0.5)
OCC5	0.055	(0.2)	0.171	(0.5)
CONSTANT	−1.719	(7.1)	−1.519	(7.7)

t values in parentheses

Appendix C   Family Income Scale

A scale of family income was constructed for the British women from the information of the socio-economic groups of the husband's occupation at the 1980 WES interview and their earnings, where available. There was a large amount of missing data on husbands' earnings. A cross-tabulation of socio-economic group and earnings by age of the husband provided a ranking of socio-economic groups by average earnings, and socio-economic groups were then allocated to a five-point ranked family income scale. The five categories are described below, using husband's socio-economic group at the interview starting from the lowest:

Category 1   All non-working and information unavailable. Assumed to be lowest income group. This may be an unrealistic assumption but there is no way of checking.

Category 2   Socio-economic groups 7, 10, 11, 14, or 15, that is, personal service, semi-skilled manual, unskilled manual, farmers (own account) and agricultural workers.

Category 3   Socio-economic groups 6, 8 and 9, that is, junior non-manual, foreman and supervisors, skilled manual.

Category 4   Socio-economic groups 5, 12, 13 and 17, that is, intermediate non-manual, own account (not professional) farmers, employers, managers, inadequately described.

Category 5   Socio-economic groups 1, 2, 3 or 4, that is, employers, managers of large and small establishments, professional self-employed, professional employees.

Various alternative and more extended groupings of these occupations were constructed but they made little difference to the results. This scale was used as the FAMINC variable in the regression analysis on the timing of the first return to work after childbirth in Chapter 3.

References

Adams, C. T. and Winston, K. T. (1980) *Mothers at work: Public Policies in the United States, Sweden and China* (Longman, New York and London).

All States Tax Guide (1984) (Prentice-Hall, Englewood Cliffs, NJ).

Applebaum, E. (1981) *Back to Work* (Auburn Press) 1981.

Armstrong, P. (1982) 'If It's Only Women It Doesn't Matter So Much', in West, J. (ed.) *Work, Women and the Labour Market* (Routledge & Kegan Paul, London).

Bacon, R. and Eltis, W. A. (1976) *Britain's Economic Problem: Too Few Producers* (Macmillan, London).

Beck, E. M., Horan, P. M. and Tolbert, C. M. (1978) 'Stratification in a Dual Economy: A Sectoral Model of Earnings Determination', *American Sociological Review*, 43, pp. 704–20.

Beck, R. (1982) 'Beyond the Stalemate in Child Care Public Policy', in *Day Care: Scientific and Social Policy Issues*, eds, E. F. Zigler and E. W. Gordon (Auburn House, Boston, Massachusetts).

✗ Beechey, V. (1977) 'Some Notes on Female Wage Labour in Capitalist Production', *Capital and Class*, 3, pp. 45–66.

Bell, C., McKee, L. and Priestly, K. (1983) *Fathers, Childbirth and Work* (Equal Opportunities Commission: Manchester).

Bell, D. (1974) *The Coming of Post-industrial Society: A Venture in Social Forecasting* (Heinemann: London).

Beller, A. H. (1979) 'The Impact of Equal Opportunity Laws on the Male–Female Earnings Differential', in *Women in the Labor Market*, eds, B. Lloyd, S. Andrews, and C. L. Gilroy (Columbia University Press: New York).

Beller, A. H. (1980) 'The Effect of Economic Conditions on the Success of Equal Employment Opportunity Laws: An Application to the Sex Differential in Earnings', *Review of Economics and Statistics*, 62: August, pp. 379–87.

Beller, A. H. (1982) 'Occupational Segregation by Sex: Determinants and Changes', *Journal of Human Resources*, vol. XVII, no. 3, pp. 371–92.

Beller, A. H. (1982a) 'Trends in Occupational Segregation by Sex', working papers in Population Studies no. Ps 8203 (School of Social Sciences, University of Illinois, Urbana-Champaign).

Blackaby, F. (ed.) (1978) *De-industrialisation* (Heinemann/National Institute of Economic and Social Research, London).

Blau, F. (1978) 'The Impact of the Unemployment Rate on Labor Force Entries and Exits' in *Women's Changing Roles at Home and on the Job*. (National Commission for Manpower Policy, Washington) Special Report N. 26.

Blau, F. and Henricks, W. E. (1979) 'Occupational Segregation by Sex: Trends and Prospects', *Journal of Human Resources*, 14, pp. 197–210.

Blinder, A. S. (1973) 'Wage Discrimination: Reduced Form and Structural Estimates', *Journal of Human Resources*, Fall, pp. 436–55.

Bone, M. (1977) *Pre-school Children and the Need for Day-care* (HMSO, London).

Bridges, W. P. (1980) 'Industry Marginality and Female Employment: A New Appraisal', *American Sociology Review*, vol. 45, pp. 58–75.

Browne, A. C. (1984) 'The Mixed Economy of Day Care: Consumer versus Professional Assessments', *Journal of Social Policy*, 13.3, pp. 321–31.

Bruegel, I. (1979) 'Women as a Reserve Army: A Note on Recent British Experience', *Feminist Review* 3.

Chiplin, B., Curran, M. M. and Parsley, C. J. (1980) 'Relative Female Earnings in Great Britain and the Impact of Legislation', in Sloane, P. (ed.) *Women and Low Pay* (Macmillan, London).

Chiplin, B. and Sloane, P. J. (1982) *Tackling Discrimination at the Work Place: An Analysis of Sex Discrimination in Britain* (Cambridge University Press: Cambridge).

Corcoran, M. E. (1979) 'Work Experience, Labor Force Withdrawals and Women's Wages: Empirical Results Using the 1976 Panel of Income Dynamics', in Lloyd, C. B. *et al*, *Women in the Labor Market* (Columbia University Press, New York).

Corcoran, M. E. and Duncan, G. H. (1979) 'Work History, Labor Force Attachment, and Earnings Differences between Races and Sexes', *Journal of Human Resources* vol. XIV, no. 1, pp. 1–20.

Davidson, M. J. and Cooper, C. L. (1983) 'Working Women in the European Community – The Future Prospect', *Long Range Planning*, vol. 16, no. 4, pp. 49–54.

Dex, S. (1983) *Women's Work Histories, Part II*, Report to Department of Employment, London, unpublished.

Dex, S. (1984) *Women's Work Histories*, Department of Employment, Research Paper no. 46.

Dex, S. (1984a) 'Women's Occupational Profiles', *Employment Gazette*, vol. 92, no. 12.

Dex, S. and Perry, S. P. (1984) 'Women's Employment Changes in the 1970s', *Employment Gazette*, 92, no. 4, pp. 151–64.

Dolton, P. J. and Makepeace, G. H. (1984) 'Sample Selection and Male-Female Earnings Differentials in the Graduate Labour Market', Hull Economic Research Papers no. 117.

Edwards, R. C., Reich, M. and Gordon, D. M. (eds) (1975) *Labor Market Segmentation* (D. C. Heath, Lexington: Massachusetts).

Ehrlich, H. J. *et al.* (1975) *Women and Men: A Socioeconomic Fact Book* (Vacant Lots Press, Baltimore, Maryland).

Eisner, R. (1978) 'Employment Taxes and Subsidies', *Work Time and Employment* (National Commission for Employment Policy, US Government Printing Office: Washington) Special Report no. 28.

Elias, P. (1983) *Occupational Mobility and Part-time Work*, Institute for Employment Research, University of Warwick (mimeo).

England, P. (1982) 'The Failure of Human Capital Theory to Explain

Occupational Sex Segregation', *Journal of Human Resources*, vol. XVII, no. 3, pp. 358–70.

Equal Opportunities Commission (1978) *I Want to Work . . . but What About the Kids?* (EOC, Manchester).

Equal Opportunities Commission (1984) *Equal Pay for Work of Equal Value: An Outline of the Amended Equal Pay Act* (EOC, Manchester).

Felmlee, D. H. (1982) 'Women's Job Mobility, Processes Within and Between Employers', *American Sociological Review*, vol. 47, pp. 142–51.

Freeman, R. B. (1984) 'Affirmative Action: Good, Bad, or Irrelevant', *New Perspectives*, 16, US Commission on Civil Rights, Fall, pp. 23–7.

Gershuny, J. (1978) *After Industrial Society? The Emerging Self-service Economy* (Macmillan, London).

Glucklich, P., Povall, M., Snell, M. W. and Zell, A. (1981) *Equal Pay and Opportunity*, (Department of Employment, London) Research Paper no. 20.

Goldstein, M. and Smith, R. S. (1976) 'The Estimated Impact of the Anti-discrimination Program Aimed at Federal Contractors', *Industrial and Labor Relations Review*, 29: July, pp. 523–43.

Gordon, N. M. (1979) 'Institutional Responses: The Federal Income Tax System', in *The Subtle Revolution*, (ed.) E. Smith (The Urban Institute, Washington).

Gross, E. (1968) '*Plus ça change. . .*? The Sexual Structure of Occupations over Time', *Social Problems*, 16, pp. 198–208.

Hakim, C. (1979) *Occupational Segregation* (Department of Employment, London) Research Paper no. 9.

Hakim, C (1981) 'Job Segregation: Trends in the 1970s', *Employment Gazette*, December, pp. 521–9.

Heckman, J. (1974) 'Effects of Child Care Programs on Women's Work Effort', *Journal of Political Economy*, 82, pp. 5136–63.

Heckman, J. J. and Wolpin, K. I. (1976) 'Does the Contract Compliance Program Work: An Analysis of Chicago Data', *Industrial and Labor Relations Review*, 29: July, pp. 544–64.

Iams, H. M. and Thornton, A. (1975) 'Decomposition of Differences: A Cautionary Note', *Sociological Methods and Research*, February, pp. 341–51.

Joseph, G. (1983) *Women at Work: The British Experience* (Philip Allan, Oxford).

Joshi, H. E. (1984) *Women's Participation in Paid Work: Further Analysis of the Women and Employment Survey* (Department of Employment, London) Research Paper no. 45.

Joshi, H. E. and Newell, M. L. (1985) 'Parenthood and Pay Differences: Evidence from the MRC National Survey of Health and Development of the 1946 Birth Cohort', Report to the Department of Employment, February.

Jusenius, C. L. (1976) 'The Influence of Work Experience and Typicality of Occupational Assignment on Women's Earnings', *Dual Careers*, vol. 4, US Department of Labor, Employment and Training Administration monograph, no. 21.

Kahne, H., Kohen, A. I. and Hurley, D. S. (1975) 'Economic Perspectives on the Roles of Women in the American Economy', *Journal of Economic Literature*, vol. XII, no. 4, pp. 1249–92.

Killingsworth, M. R. (1979) 'Comment', *Women in the Labor Market* (eds) B. Lloyd, E. S. Andrews and C. L. Gilroy (Columbia University Press: New York).

Leonard, J. S. (1984) 'Antidiscrimination or Reverse Discrimination: The Impact of Changing Demographics, Title VII, and Affirmative Action on Productivity', *Journal of Human Resources*, 19, Spring, pp. 145–74.

Leonard, J. S. (1984a) 'Employment and Occupational Advance under Affirmative Action', *Review of Economics and Statistics*, 66, August, pp. 377–85.

Leonard, J. S. (1984b) 'The Impact of Affirmative Action on Employment', *Journal of Labour Economics*, 2: October, pp. 439–63.

Leonard, J. S. (1985) 'What Promises Are Worth: The Impact of Affirmative Action Goals', *Journal of Human Resources*, 20, Winter, pp. 3–20.

Levine, J. A. (1981) 'Child Care and Equal Employment Opportunity for Women', report prepared for the US Commission on Civil Rights, June.

Long, J. G. and Jones, G. B. (1980) 'Labor Force Entry and Exit by Married Women: A Longitudinal Analysis', *The Review of Economics and Statistics*, LXII, no. 1, pp. 1–6.

Low, S. and Spindler, P. (1968) *Child Care Arrangements of Working Mothers in the United States* (US Department of Labor: The Women's Bureau, Washington, D.C.).

Macke, A. S., Hudis, P. M. and Larrick, D. (1978) 'Sex Role Attitudes and Employment among Women: a Dynamic Model of Continuity and Change' in *Women's Changing Roles at Home and on the Job* (ed.) Isabel Sawhill, National Commission on Employment Policy, Special Report no. 26.

Martin, J. and Roberts, C. (1984) *Women and Employment: A Lifetime Perspective* (DE/OPCS, HMSO, London).

Meehan, E. M. (1985) *Women's Rights at Work: Campaigns and Policy in Britain and the United States* (Macmillan, London)

Morgan, J. N. (1980) 'Child Care When Parents Work', *Five Thousand American Families*, vol. IX.

Morgan, W. (forthcoming) 'Returning to School at Midlife', in *Dual Careers*, vol. 6 (ed.) L. B. Shaw Report to the US Department of Labor.

Mott, F. L. (ed.) (1982) *The Employment Revolution: Young American Women of the 1970s* (MIT Press, Cambridge).

Mott, F. L. and Shapiro, D. (1982) 'Continuity of Work Attachment Among New Mothers' in Mott, 1982.

National Center for Education Statistics (1980) *The Condition of Education* (US Government Printing Office, Washington, DC).

National Union of Teachers (1973) *The Provision of Pre-school Education in England and Wales* (NUT, London).

Oaxaca, R. L. (1973) 'Male–Female Wage Differentials in Urban Labor Markets', *International Economic Review*, October, pp. 693–709.

Oppenheimer, V. K. (1970) *The Female Labor force in the US* (Population Monograph Series no. 5, Berkeley, California).

Osterman, P. (1982) 'Affirmative Action and Opportunity: A Study of Female Quit Rates', *Review of Economics and Statistics*, 64, November, pp. 604–12.

Pike, M. (1984) 'The Employment Response to Equal Pay Legislation', Labour Economics Unit no. 2, University of Hull.

Pindyke, R. S. and Rubinfeld, D. L. (1976) *Econometric models and economic forecasts* (McGraw-Hill, Maidenhead).

Piore, M. J. (1975) 'Notes for a Theory of Labor Market Stratification' in Edwards, Reich and Gordon (eds.).

Rhoton, P. (1984) 'Attrition and the Longitudinal Surveys of Labor Force Behaviour', *IASSIST Quarterly* (International Surveys for Social Science Information Service and Technology) vol. 8, no. 2, pp. 2–16.

Robinson, O. and Wallace, J. (1984) *Part-time Employment and Sex Discrimination Legislation in Great Britain* (Department of Employment, London) Research Paper no. 43.

Rosenfeld, R. A. (1979) 'Women's Occupational Careers: Individual and Structural Explanations', *Sociology of Work and Occupations*, vol. 6, no. 3, pp. 283–311.

Rosenfeld, R. A. (1980) 'Race and Sex Differences in Career Dynamics', *American Sociological Review*, 45.4, pp. 583–609.

Sandell, S. H. and Shapiro, D. (1978) 'The Theory of Human Capital and the Earnings of Women: A Re-examination of the Evidence', *Journal of Human Resources*, 13, pp. 103–17.

Sawhill, I. (1979) 'Comment', in *Women in the Labor Market*, eds C. B. Lloyd, E. S. Andrews and C. L. Gilroy (Columbia University Press, New York).

Shaeffer, R. G. and Lynton, E. F. (1979) *Corporate Experiences in Improving Women's Job Opportunities* (The Conference Board, New York).

Shapiro, D. and Shaw, L. B. (1983) 'Growth in the Labor Force Attachment of Married Women: Accounting for Changes in the 1970s', *Southern Economic Journal*, October, pp. 461–73.

Shaw, L. B. (1983) 'Problems of Labor Market Re-entry', in Shaw, L. B. (1983) *Unplanned careers: The Working Lives of Middle-aged Women* (D. C. Heath, Lexington, Massachusetts).

Shaw, L. B. (1983a) 'Does Working Part-time Contribute to Women's Occupational Segregation?', paper presented to the annual meeting of the Midwest Economic Association, St Louis, Missouri, April 1983, mimeo, unpublished.

Shaw L. B. (1984) 'Effects of Education and Occupational Training on the Wages of Mature Women', Special Report to the US Department of Labor, Washington, DC.

Shaw, L. B. (1985) 'Child Care Policy in the United States of America', paper presented at a workshop on child-care policy (Equal Opportunities Commission, London).

Shaw, L. B. and O'Brien, T. (1983) 'Introduction and Overview', in Shaw, 1983.

Sleeper, R. A. (1975) 'Industrial Mobility and the Life Cycle', *British Journal of Industrial Relations*.

Smith-Lovin, L. and Tickamyer, A. R. (1981) 'Fertility and Patterns of

Labor Force Participation among Married Women', *Social Biology*, 28, pp. 81–95.

Sorensen, A. (1983) 'Children and their Mothers', *Social Science Research*, 12, pp. 26–43.

Sorensen, A. (1983a) 'Women's Employment Patterns after Marriage', *Journal of Marriage and the Family*, May, pp. 311–21.

Sorensen, A. B. (1977) 'The Structure of Inequality and the Process of Attainment', *American Sociological Review*, 42, pp. 965–78.

Spilerman, S. (1977) 'Careers, Labor Market Structures and Socio-economic Achievement', *American Journal of Sociology*, 83, pp. 51–93.

Statham, A. and Rhoton, P. (1983) 'Attitudes towards Women Working: Changing over Time and Implications for the Labor-Force Behaviours of Husbands and Wives' in Shaw, 1983.

Stewart, M. and Greenhalgh, C. A. (1982) 'The Training and Experience Dividend', *Employment Gazette*, August, pp. 329–40.

Stewart, M. and Greenhalgh, C. A. (1984) 'Work History Patterns and Occupational Attainment of Women', *The Economic Journal*, 94, no. 375, pp. 493–519.

Thatcher, A. R. (1978) 'Labour Supply and Employment Trends' in Blackaby, F. (ed.) (1978).

Tuma, N. B. (1976) 'Rewards, resources, and the rate of mobility: A non-stationary multivariate stochastic model', *American Sociological Review*, 41, pp. 338–60.

Tuma, N. B. and Hannan, M. T. (1978) 'Approaches to the Censoring Problem in Analysis of Event Histories', in Schuessler, K. F. (ed.) *Sociological Methodology* (Jossey Bass: San Francisco).

Tzannatos, P. Z. and Zabalza, A. (1984) 'The Anatomy of the Rise of British Female Relative Wages in the 1970s: Evidence from the New Earnings Survey', *British Journal of Industrial Relations*, pp. 177–94.

US Bureau of the Census (1983) 'Child Care Arrangements of Working Mothers: June 1982', *Current Population Reports*, Series P–23, no. 129 (US Government Printing Office: Washington, DC).

US Department of Labor (1975) *1975 Handbook on Women Workers*, Employment Standards Administration Women's Bureau (US Department of Labor, Washington DC).

US Department of the Treasury (1975) *1975 Federal Income Tax Forms* (Internal Revenue Service, Washington DC).

Wachter, M. (1972) 'A Labor Supply Model for Secondary Workers', *Review of Economics and Statistics*, 54, pp. 141–51.

Waite, J. (1979) 'Projection of Female Labor Force Participation from Sex-role Attitudes' in *Women in the Labor Force in 1990*, R. E. Smith (ed.) (The Urban Institute, Washington, DC).

Wallace, P. (1979) 'Comment', in *Women in the Labor Market*, eds C. B. Lloyd, E. S. Andrews and C. L. Gilroy (Columbia University Press, New York).

Wallace, P. A. (ed.) (1976) *Equal Employment Opportunity and the AT & T Case* (The MIT Press, Cambridge and London).

Williams, G. (1976) 'Trends in Occupational Differentiation by Sex', *Sociology of Work Occupations*, 3, no. 1, pp. 38–62.

Winget, W. (1982) 'The Dilemma of Affordable Child Care', in *Day Care: Scientific and Policy Issues*, eds E. F. Zigler and E. W. Gordon (Auburn House, Boston).

Zigler, E. F. and Goodman, J. (1982) 'The Battle for Day Care in America: A View from the Trenches', in *Day Care: Scientific and Policy Issues*, eds E. F. Zigler and E. W. Gordon (Auburn House, Boston).

Index